THE BEGINNING OF BRUCE: HOW THE BIG BOSS LAUNCHED A MARTIAL ARTS PHENOMENON

In 1971, the world of cinema witnessed a seismic shift with the release of The Big Boss, a film that would not only introduce audiences to the unparalleled talent of Bruce Lee but also forever alter the landscape of martial arts films. Prior to this film, Bruce Lee was relatively unknown to international audiences, his remarkable skills and charisma largely confined to television and minor film roles. However, with The Big Boss, Lee's magnetic screen presence and revolutionary fighting style catapulted him to stardom, marking the beginning of an extraordinary career that would establish him as a global icon. This film, steeped in action and intensity, was more than just a commercial success; it became a cultural milestone, laying the foundation for the martial arts phenomenon that would sweep across the globe. The Big Boss was not just the start of Bruce Lee's legendary journey, but the spark that ignited a worldwide passion for martial arts cinema.

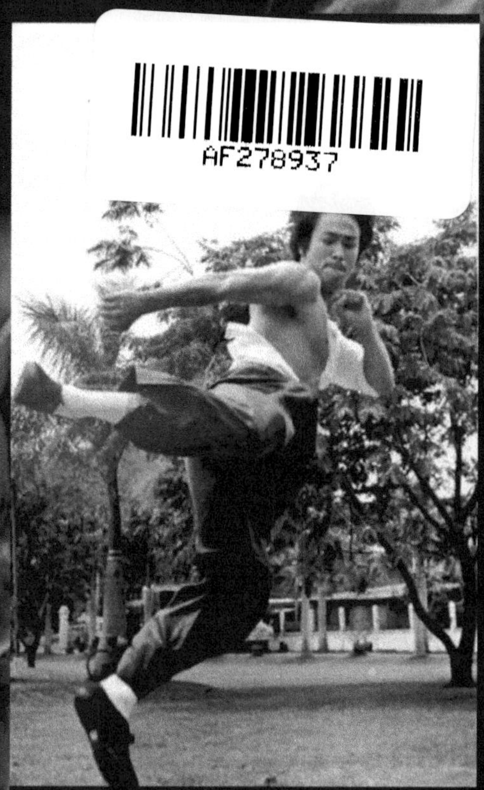

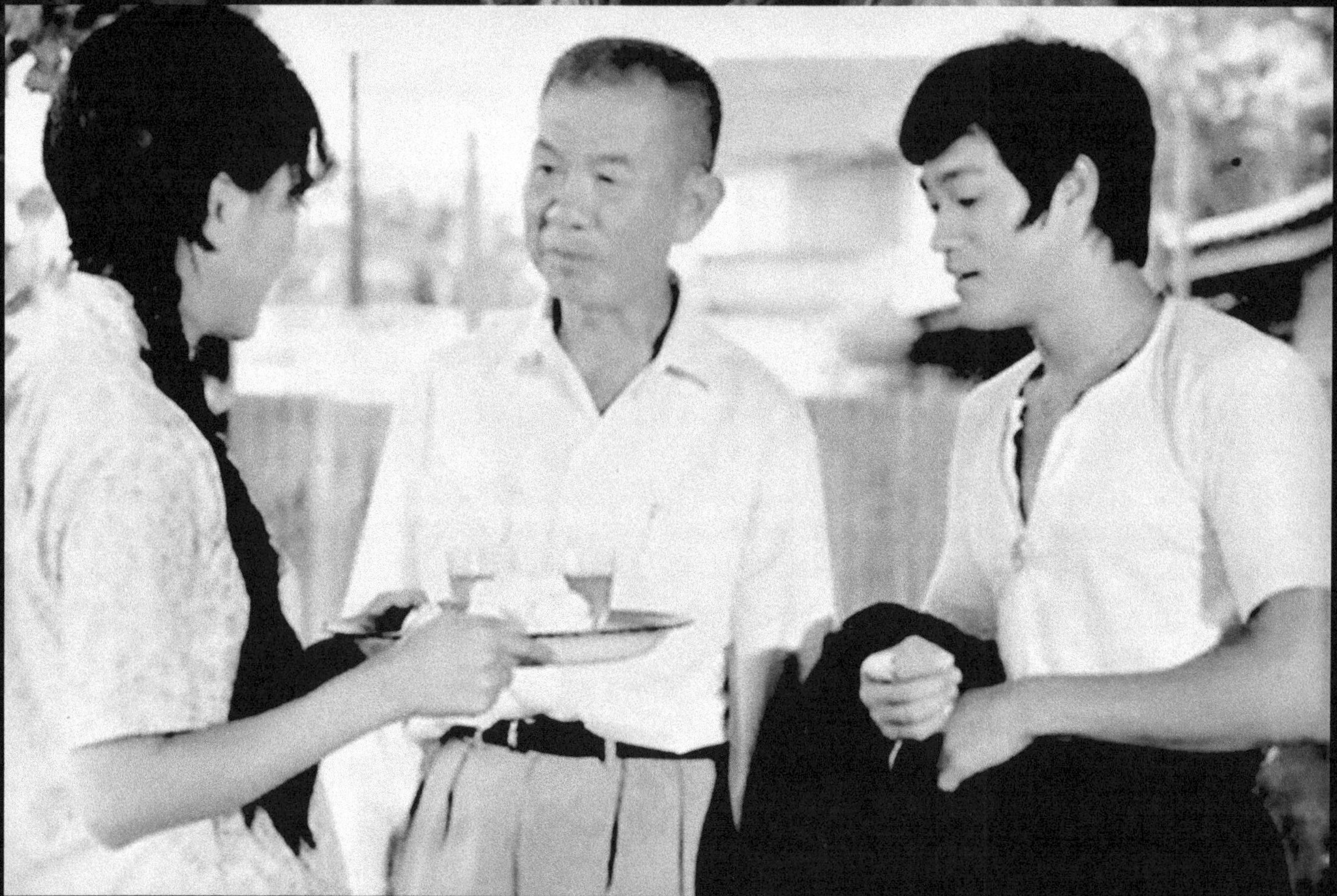

ブルースの始まり：『ドラゴン危機一発』がいかにして武道の現象を生み出したか

1971年、映画界に大きな変革が訪れました。それは、ブルース・リーの並外れた才能を世に知らしめ、武術映画の世界を永遠に変えることとなった映画『ドラゴン危機一発』の公開です。この映画の公開以前、ブルース・リーは国際的な観客にはほとんど知られておらず、その驚異的な技術とカリスマ性は主にテレビや小さな映画の役に留まっていました。しかし、『ドラゴン危機一発』によって、リーの圧倒的なスクリーンプレゼンスと革命的な戦闘スタイルが一躍注目を浴び、彼をスターの座へと押し上げました。これを機に、彼は世界的なアイコンとしての地位を確立する並外れたキャリアの幕開けを迎えたのです。このアクションと緊張感に満ちた映画は、単なる商業的成功に留まらず、文化的な金字塔となり、その後、世界中に武術映画のブームを巻き起こす基盤を築きました。『ドラゴン危機一発』は、ブルース・リーの伝説的な旅の始まりであると同時に、世界的な武術映画への情熱に火をつけたきっかけとなったのです。

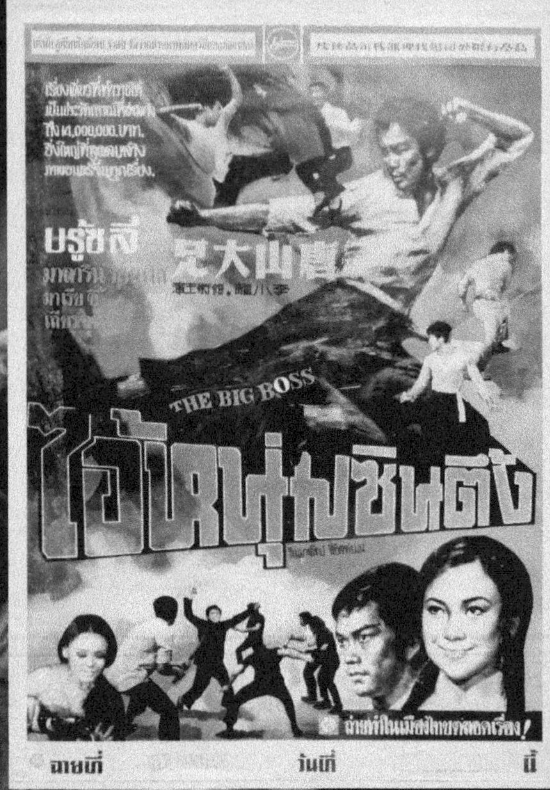

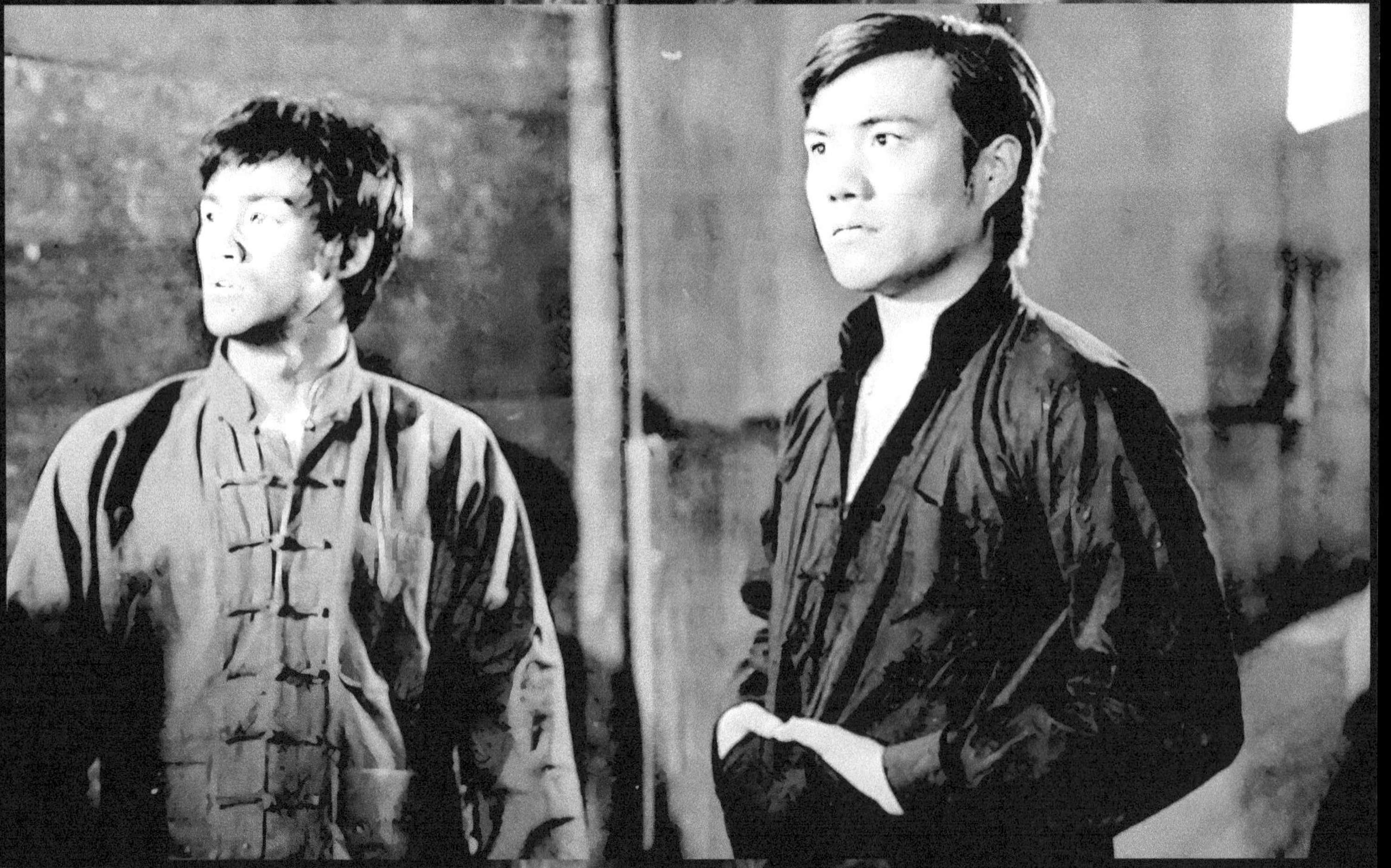

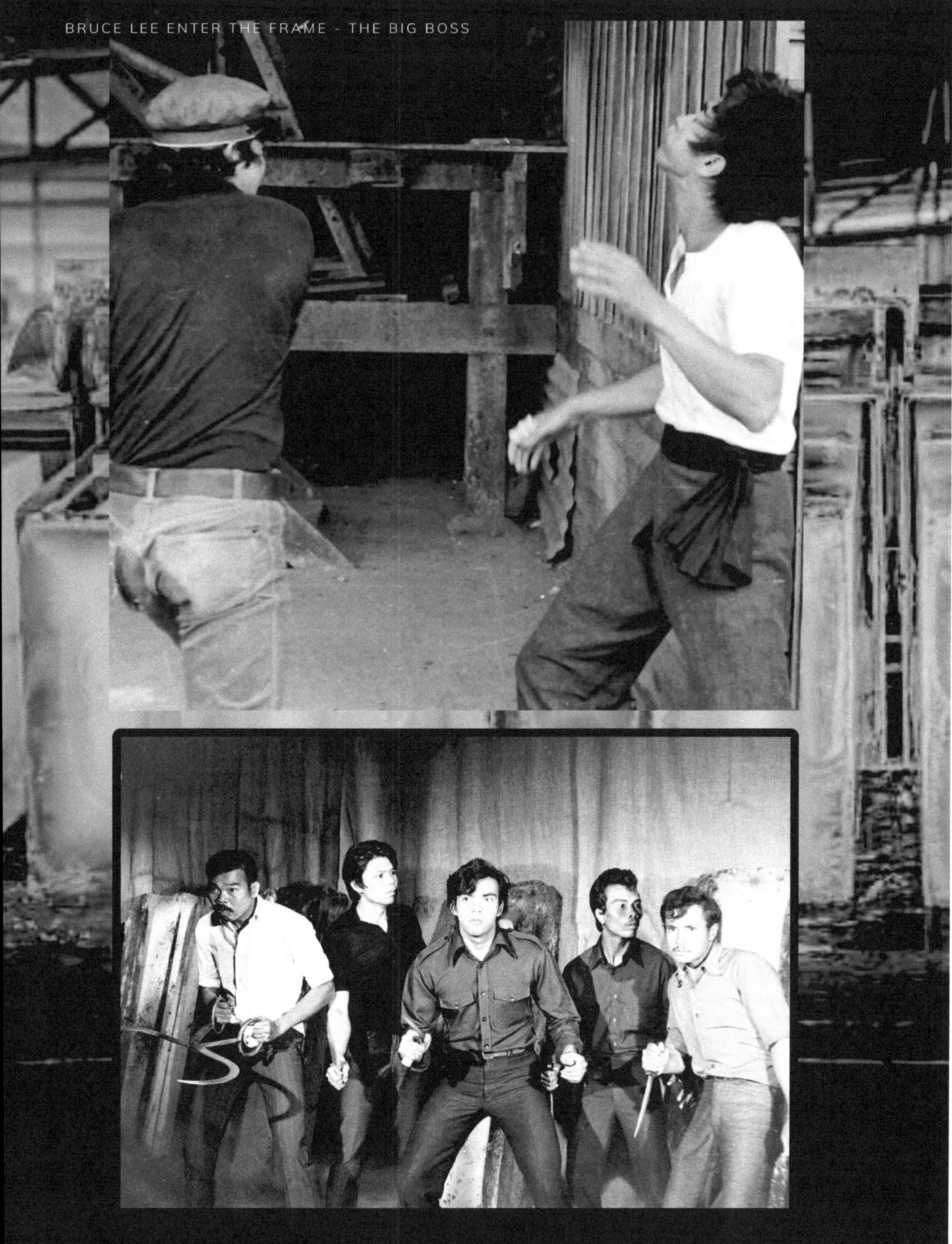

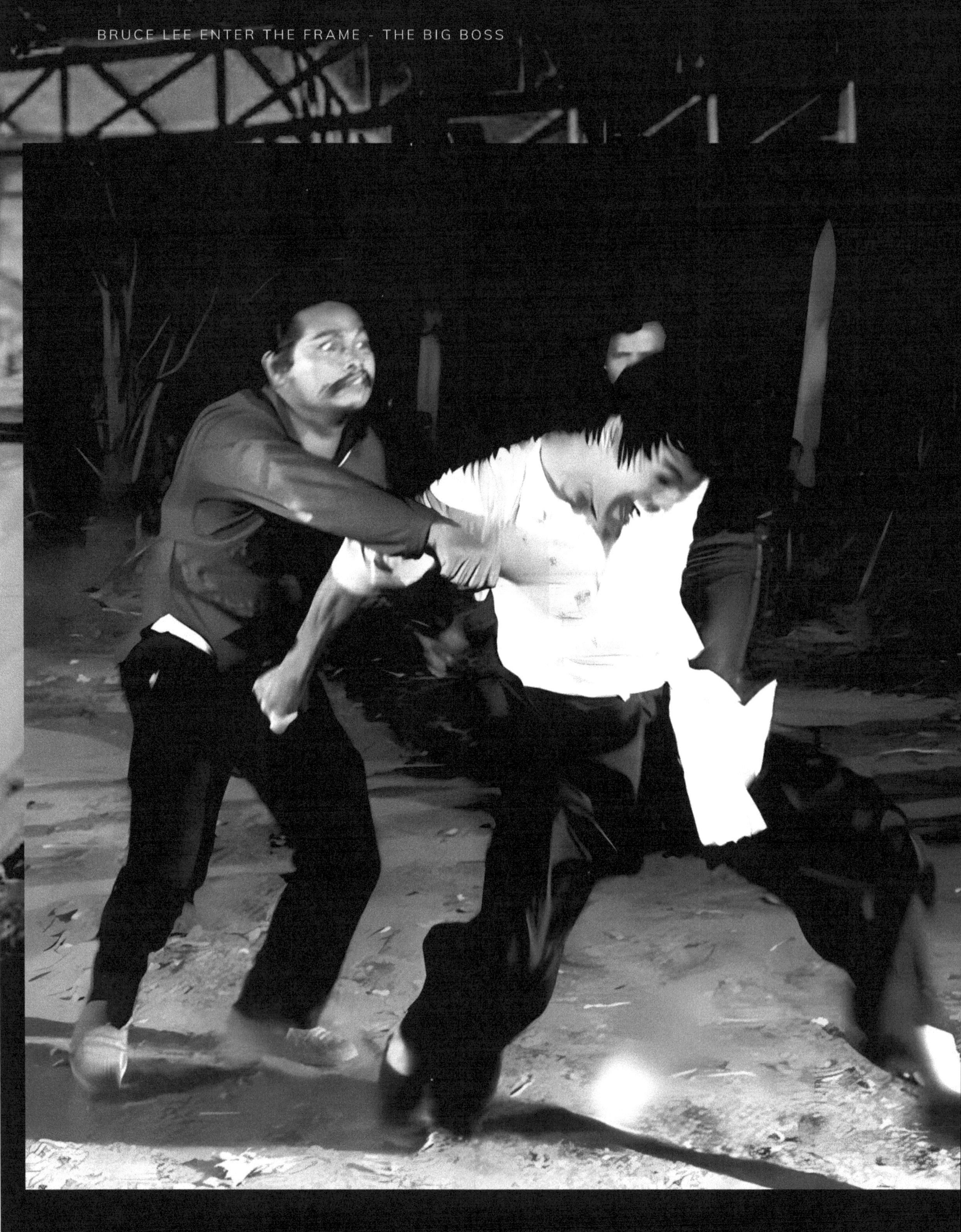

A COLD LEGACY: BRUCE LEE'S THE BIG BOSS AND THE LEGENDARY "SAW IN THE HEAD" SCENE

Over half a century has passed since the release of Bruce Lee's The Big Boss (1971), a film that not only introduced the world to a martial arts legend but also etched several unforgettable moments into the annals of cinema history. Among these moments is the iconic ice factory sequence, a scene that stands out for its intense action, and stark setting, and the mysterious "Saw in the Head" scene—a sequence that was filmed but never made it to the final cut. Today, this very ice factory in Thailand still exists, standing as a living testament to a film that changed the landscape of martial arts cinema forever.

The ice factory in The Big Boss is more than just a backdrop; it is the stage upon which Bruce Lee's character, Cheng Chao-an, unleashes his fury, marking the turning point of the film and cementing Lee's status as a global martial arts icon. Set in the town of Pak Chong, Thailand, this factory serves as the location where Lee's character, after being pushed to the limit by villainous drug smugglers, finally breaks his vow of non-violence. The raw power and precision of Lee's fighting style are on full display as he battles his way through a horde of enemies, the clattering of ice blocks and chilling atmosphere amplifying the intensity of the scene.

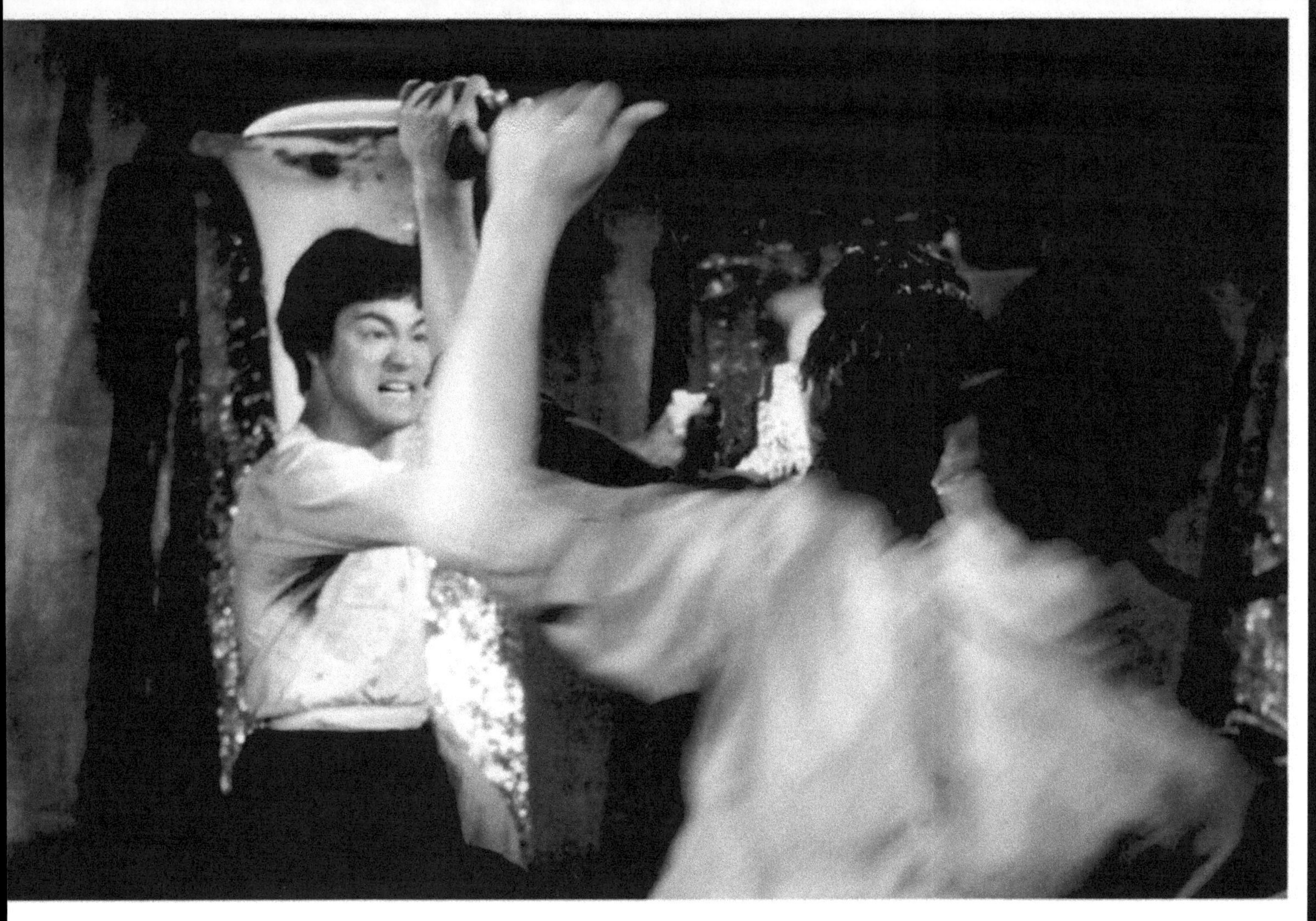

冷徹な遺産：ブルース・リーの『ドラゴン危機一発』と伝説の「頭にのこぎり」シーン

ブルース・リーの『ドラゴン危機一発』（1971年）の公開から半世紀以上が経過しました。この映画は、世界に武術の伝説を紹介しただけでなく、映画史に残るいくつもの忘れられない瞬間を刻みました。その中でも特に印象的なのが、アイスファクトリーのシーンです。激しいアクションと厳しい環境設定、そして撮影されたものの最終版には含まれなかった謎の「頭にのこぎり」シーンが、このシーンを特別なものにしています。今日、このアイスファクトリーはタイに実在し、武術映画の風景を永遠に変えた作品の生きた証として残っています。

『ドラゴン危機一発』に登場するアイスファクトリーは、単なる背景にとどまりません。ここはブルース・リー演じるチェン・チャオアンが怒りを爆発させ、映画の転換点を迎える舞台であり、彼を世界的な武術アイコンとして確立させる場所です。タイのパークチョンという町に位置するこの工場は、悪徳麻薬密売人に追い詰められたリーのキャラクターが、ついに非暴力の誓いを破る場面の舞台となります。リーの戦闘スタイルの生々しい力と精密さが余すところなく発揮され、敵の群れを打ち負かす姿は、氷塊が砕け散る音や冷たい空気感と相まって、シーンの緊迫感を一層高めています。

しかし、このシーンには謎と伝説に包まれた瞬間があります。それが悪名高い「頭にのこぎり」シーンです。様々な証言によれば、このシーンでは、ブルース・リーのキャラクターが丸ノコを使って敵の頭に刺し殺す場面が含まれていたといいます。撮影されたものの、最終版には含まれませんでした。その理由として最も信憑性があるのは二つあります。一つ目は、残酷な死を描くために使用された特殊効果が安っぽく見えてしまった可能性があること。二つ目は、プロデューサーのレイモンド・チョウが、一部地域、特にシンガポールでの検閲を懸念していたことです。シンガポールでは厳しいガイドラインにより、映画が大幅にカットされるか、あるいは上映禁止になる可能性がありました。

「頭にのこぎり」シーンは、それ以来、映画界の伝説の一部となり、その内容や重要性についてファンの間で憶測が飛び交っています。最終的にカットされたものの、このシーンが考慮された事実だけでも、当時のアクションや暴力表現の限界を押し広げた映画の大胆さを物語っています。このシーンをカットするという決定は、映画の影響を損なうものではありませんでした。それどころか、『ドラゴン危機一発』の神秘性を高め、ファンや映画史家の間で何十年にもわたる議論を巻き起こしてきたのです

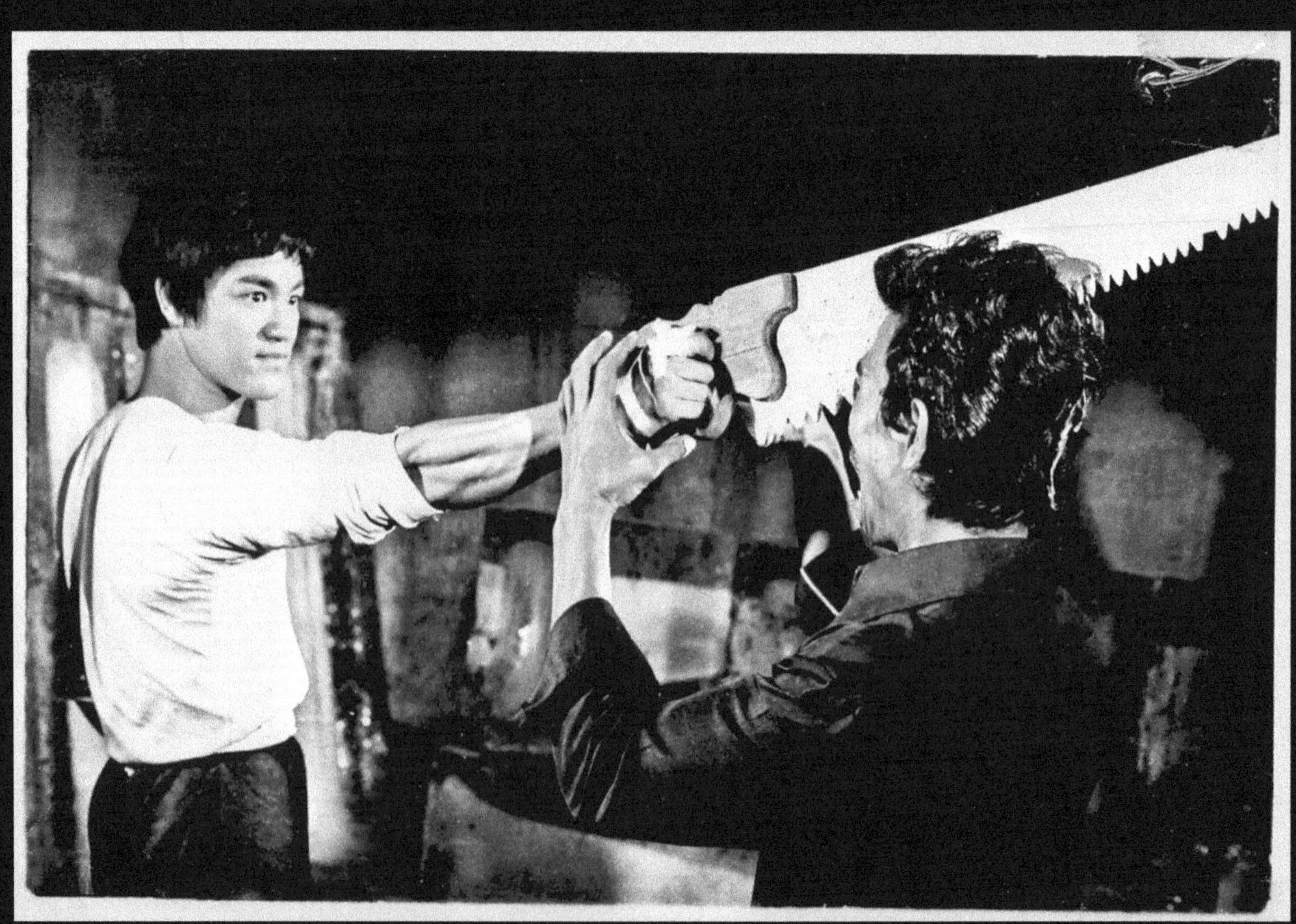

Yet, within this sequence lies a moment shrouded in mystery and legend—the infamous "Saw in the Head" scene. According to various accounts, this sequence involved Bruce Lee's character using a circular saw to kill one of his opponents by embedding it into the thug's head. Although the scene was reportedly shot, it never made it to the final version of the film. The most credible explanation for this is twofold: first, the special effects used to depict the gruesome death may have appeared too cheap and unconvincing; second, producer Raymond Chow was concerned about potential censorship in various territories, particularly in Singapore, where strict guidelines could have led to the film being heavily cut or even banned.

The "Saw in the Head" scene has since become a piece of cinematic lore, with fans speculating about its content and significance. Though it was ultimately removed, the fact that it was even considered speaks to the film's boldness in pushing the boundaries of action and violence at the time. The decision to cut the scene, however, didn't detract from the film's impact. If anything, it added to the mystique surrounding The Big Boss, fueling discussions and debates among fans and film historians for decades.

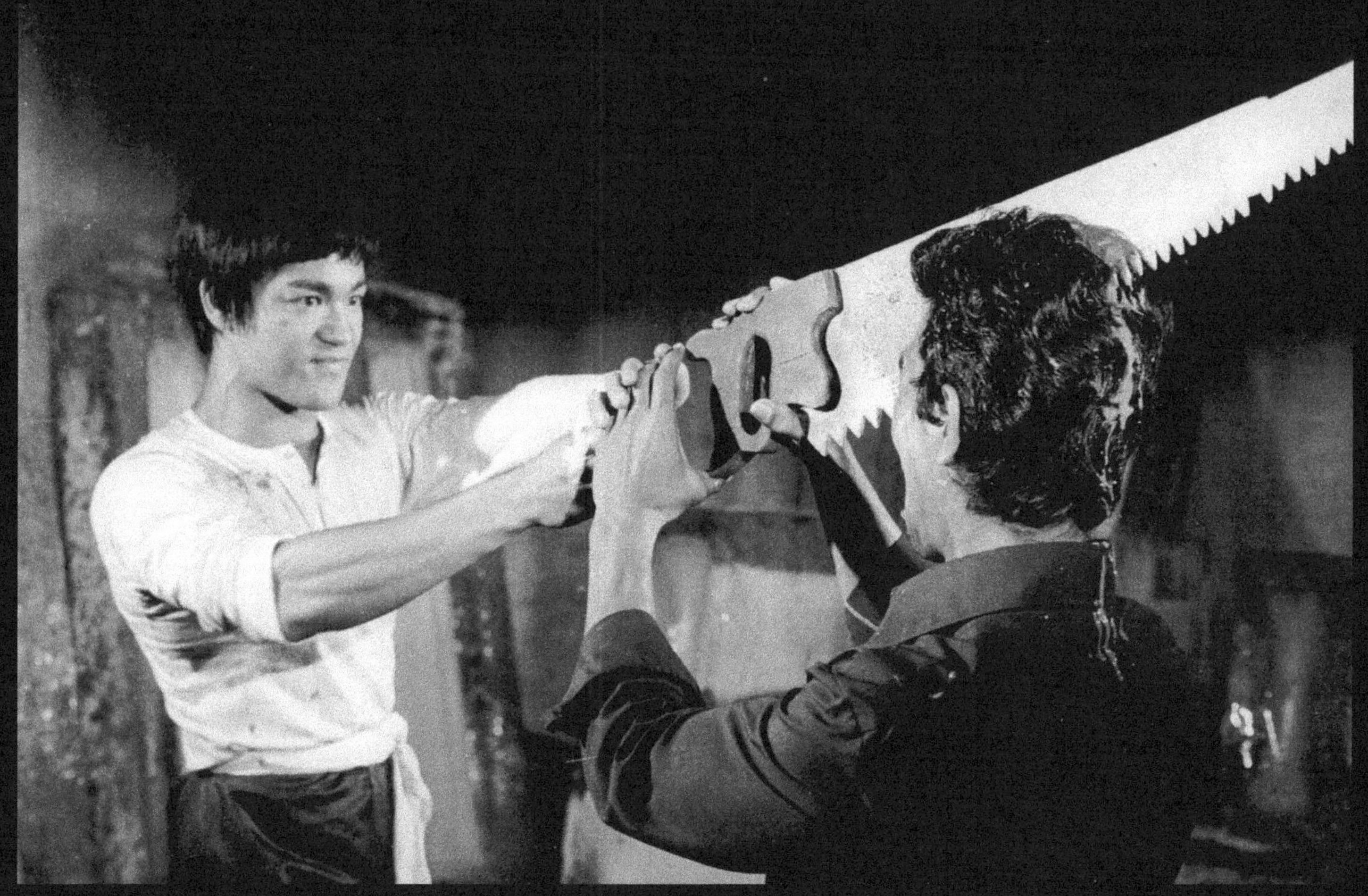

このシークエンスの中には、神秘と伝説に包まれた瞬間があります—それが悪名高い「頭にのこぎり」シーンです。さまざまな情報によれば、このシーンではブルース・リーのキャラクターが円形ののこぎりを使い、敵の頭にそれを埋め込んで殺すという内容でした。撮影されたとされるこのシーンは、最終版の映画には含まれませんでした。最も信頼性の高い説明は二つあります。一つは、残虐な死を描くための特殊効果があまりにも安っぽくて説得力に欠けていたこと、もう一つは、プロデューサーのレイモンド・チョウがさまざまな地域での検閲の可能性、特に厳しいガイドラインがあるシンガポールで映画が大幅にカットされるか、あるいは禁止される可能性を懸念していたことです。

「頭にのこぎり」シーンは、それ以降映画の伝説の一部となり、その内容と重要性についてファンたちが推測を繰り広げています。結局削除されたものの、それが検討された事実は、その時代におけるアクションと暴力の限界を押し広げる映画の大胆さを示しています。しかし、シーンの削除は映画の影響を損なうものではありませんでした。むしろ、それは『ドラゴン危機一発』を取り巻く神秘性を高め、ファンや映画史家たちの間で数十年にわたる議論や討論を促進しました。

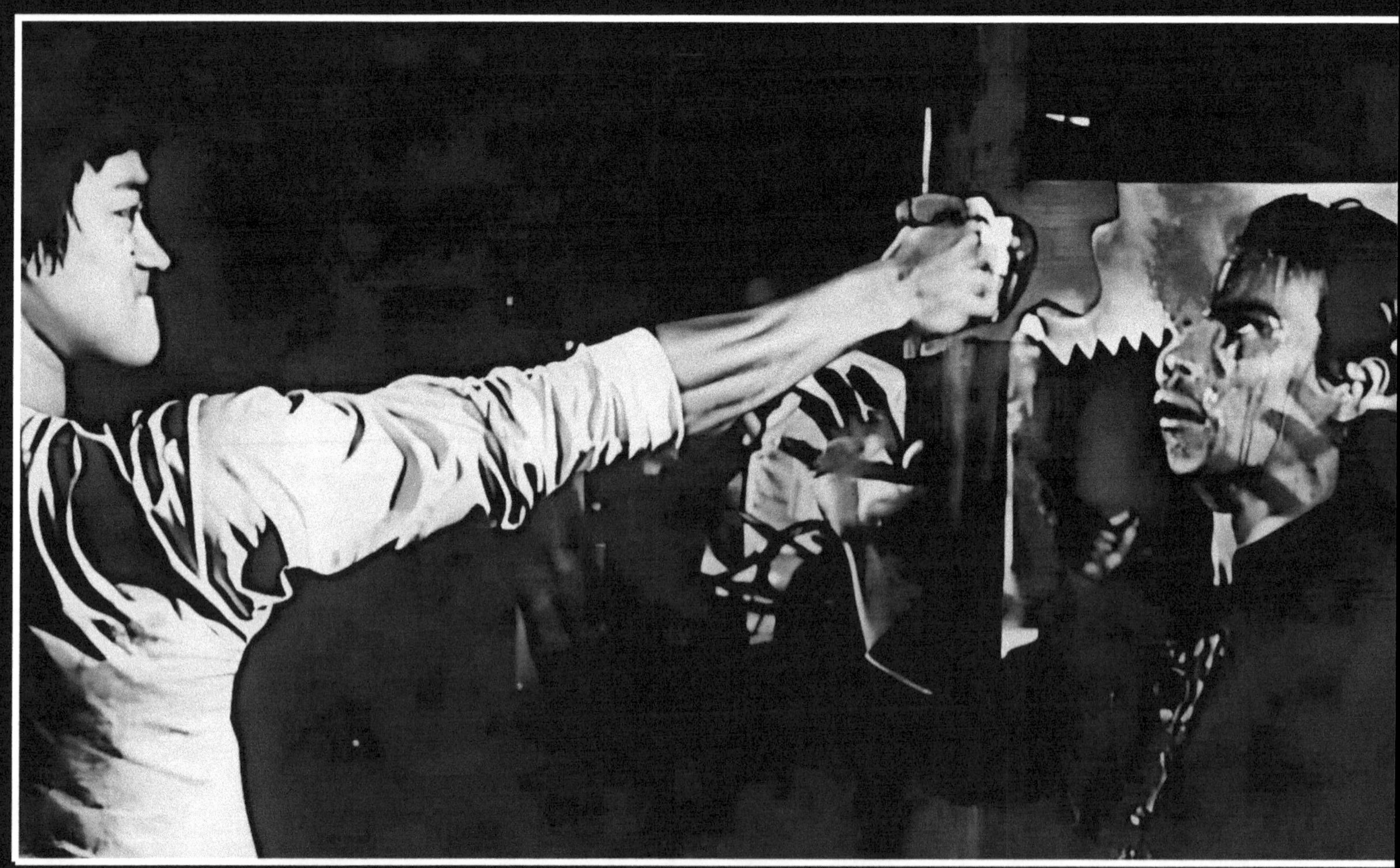

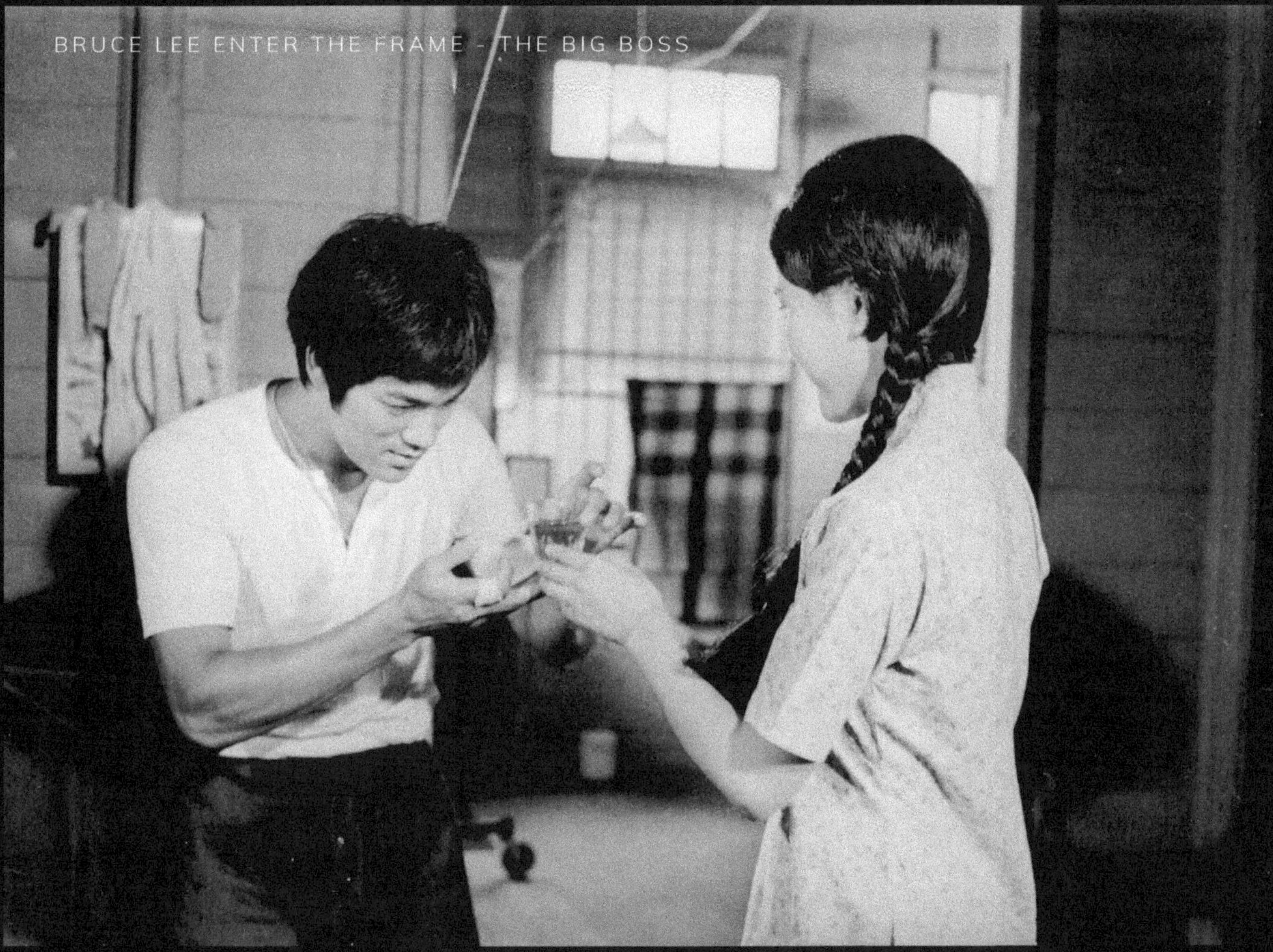

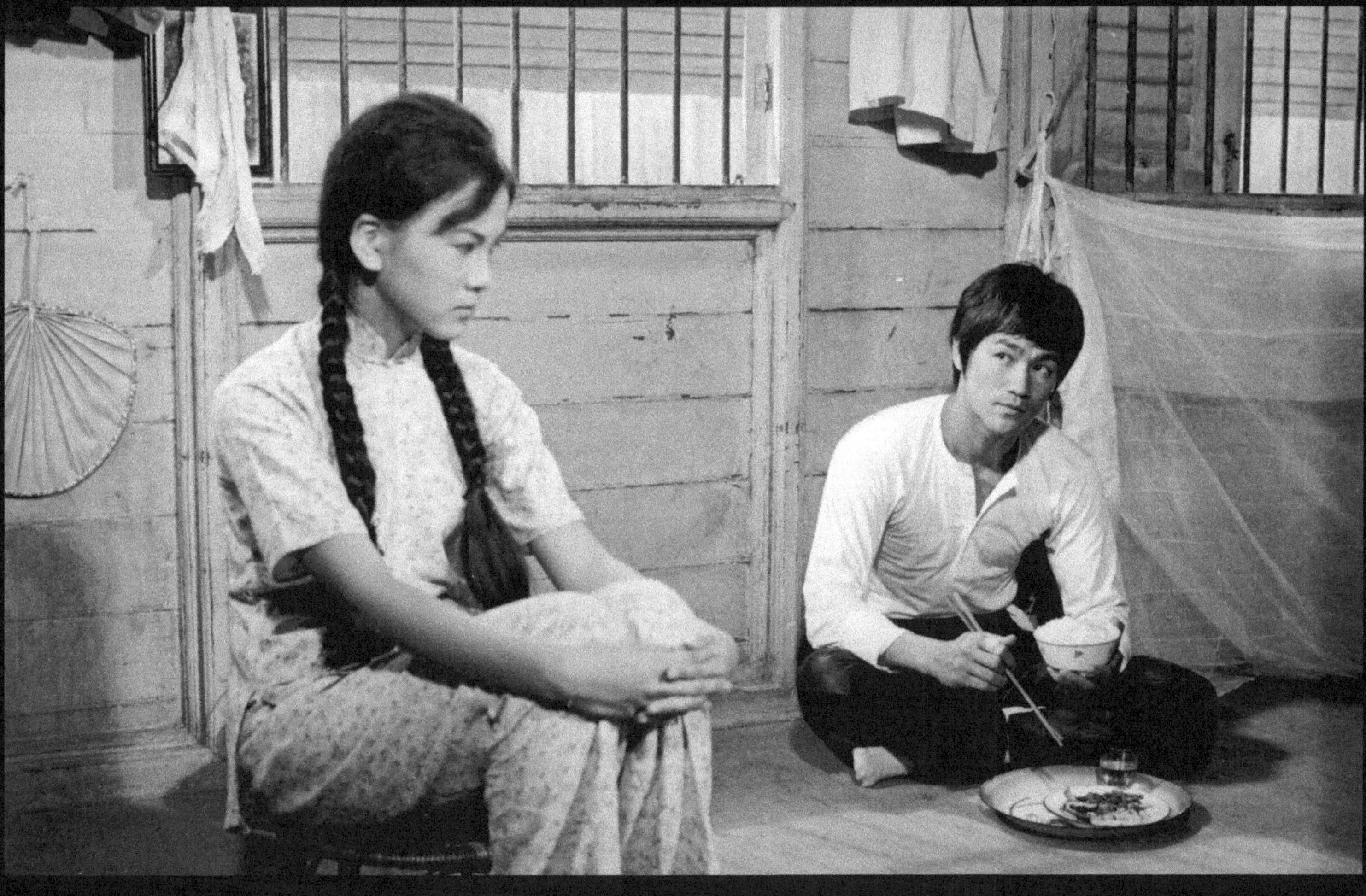

THE BIG BOSS: A PIONEERING MARTIAL ARTS MASTERPIECE

THE BIG BOSS (1971) IS MORE THAN JUST A MARTIAL ARTS FILM; IT MARKED BRUCE LEE'S EXPLOSIVE ENTRY INTO THE INTERNATIONAL FILM INDUSTRY AND SET THE STAGE FOR A REVOLUTION IN ACTION CINEMA. THIS HONG KONG PRODUCTION, DIRECTED BY LO WEI, BECAME AN ICONIC PIECE OF FILM HISTORY, FILLED WITH INTRIGUING BEHIND-THE-SCENE STORIES AND CULTURAL SIGNIFICANCE THAT RESONATE TO THIS DAY.

WHEN THE FILM WAS FIRST SCREENED IN HONG KONG, IT WASN'T JUST A MOVIE PREMIERE IT WAS A SEISMIC EVENT. THE AUDIENCE, INITIALLY STUNNED INTO SILENCE, SOON ERUPTED INTO AN UPROAR AS THEY PROCESSED THE INTENSITY OF WHAT THEY HAD JUST SEEN. THIS REACTION WAS A TESTAMENT TO THE FILM'S IMPACT, WHICH WAS UNLIKE ANYTHING THE LOCAL AUDIENCE HAD EVER EXPERIENCED.

HOWEVER, THE PATH TO THIS SUCCESS WAS ANYTHING BUT SMOOTH. BRUCE LEE, WHO WAS INITIALLY CAST AS A SECONDARY CHARACTER, WAS THRUST INTO THE LEAD ROLE AFTER THE ORIGINAL DIRECTOR, NG GAR SEUNG, WAS REPLACED BY LO WEI. THIS SWITCH ALSO ELEVATED LEE TO TOP BILLING, REPLACING JAMES TIEN, THE FILM'S ORIGINAL STAR INTERESTINGLY, THIS MIGHT EXPLAIN WHY LEE'S CHARACTER, CHENG CHAO-AN, DOESN'T ENGAGE IN COMBAT UNTIL WELL INTO THE FILM.

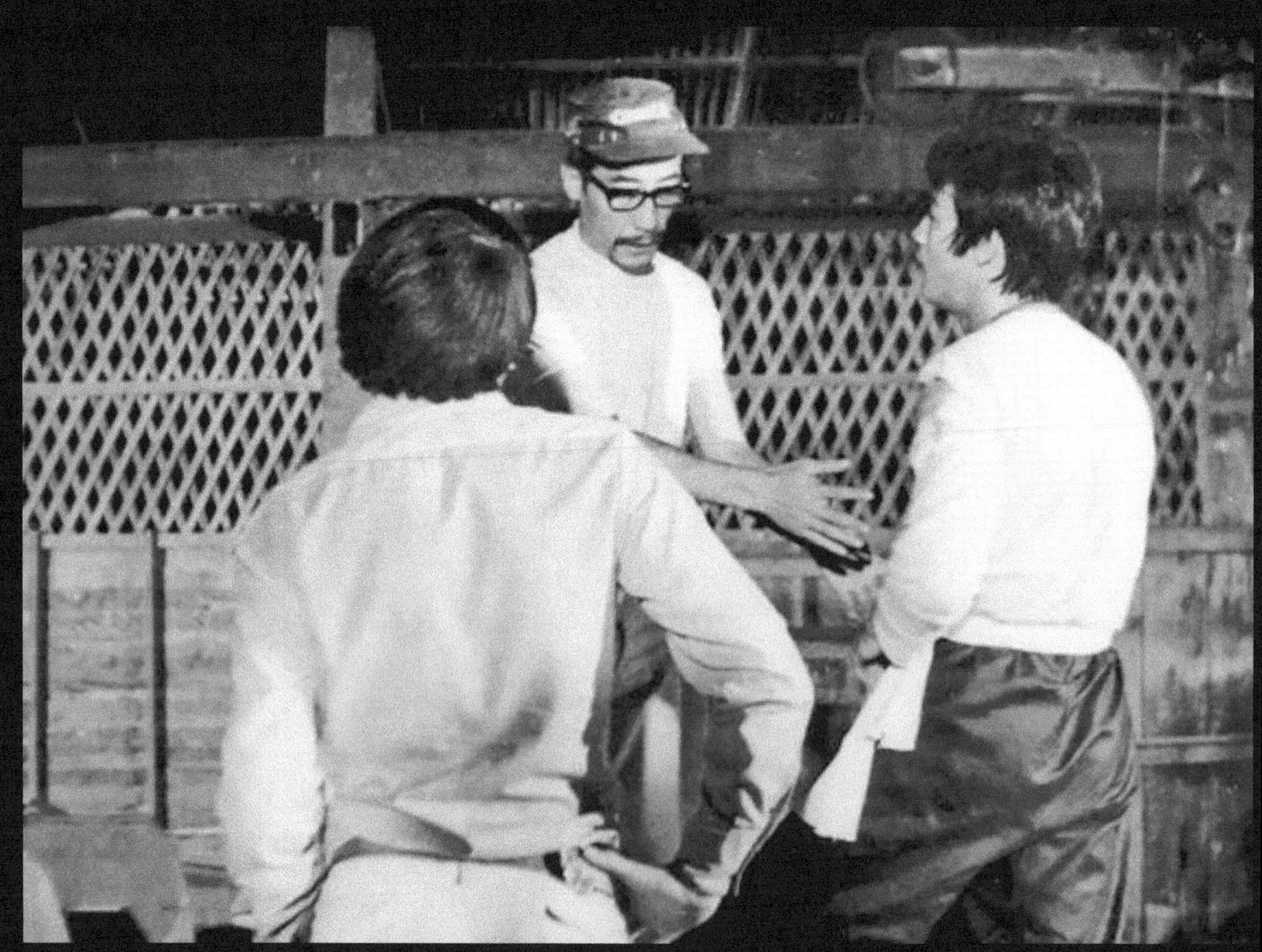

武術映画の先駆的名作『ドラゴン危機一発』

『ドラゴン危機一発』（1971年）は、単なる武術映画以上の作品です。ブルース・リーが国際映画業界に爆発的に登場し、アクション映画に革命をもたらした作品として位置付けられています。ロウ・ウェイ監督によるこの香港製作の映画は、今でも色褪せない、興味深い舞台裏のエピソードや文化的な意義に満ちた映画史のアイコン的存在となりました。

この映画が香港で初めて上映されたとき、それは単なる映画のプレミア上映ではなく、地震のような出来事でした。観客は当初、静まり返り、何が起こったのかを理解した後、突然大きな歓声が沸き起こりました。この反応は、この映画が地元の観客にとってこれまでにないほどの衝撃を与えたことを証明しています。

しかし、この成功への道のりは決して平坦ではありませんでした。ブルース・リーは当初、脇役としてキャスティングされていましたが、監督がン・ガーシェンからロウ・ウェイに交代したことで、主役に抜擢されました。この交代により、元々主演だったジェームズ・ティエンに代わってリーがトップビリングに昇格しました。興味深いことに、この交代が、リーが演じたキャラクター、チェン・チャオアンが映画の中盤まで戦闘に参加しない理由かもしれません。

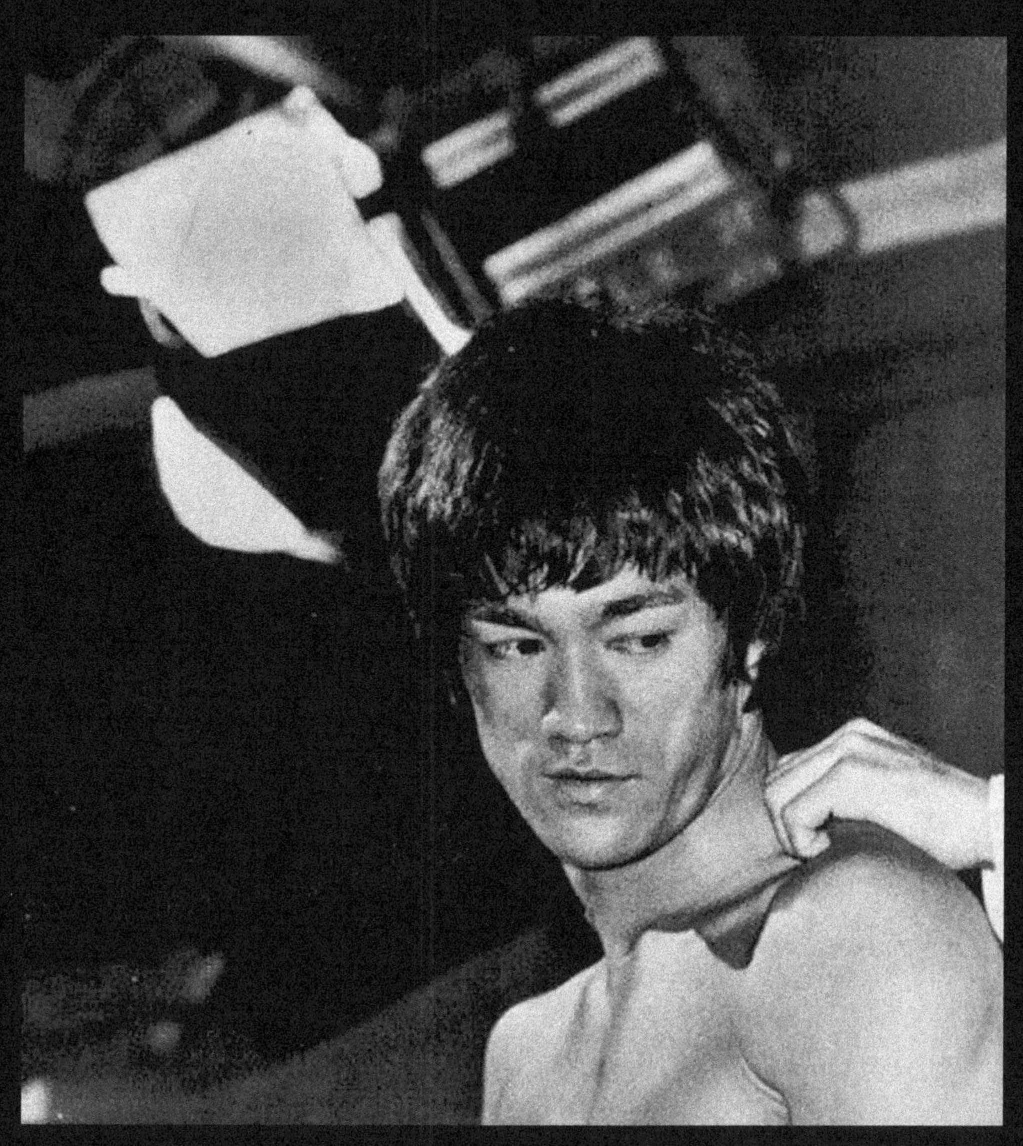

HOWEVER, THE INFLUENCE OF LEE'S AFFIRMATIONS EXTENDED FAR BEYOND HIS INITIAL BREAKTHROUGH. THE MENTAL DISCIPLINE HE CULTIVATED BECAME THE FOUNDATION FOR HIS ENTIRE PHILOSOPHY OF LIFE AND MARTIAL ARTS. LEE WAS NOT CONTENT WITH MOMENTARY SUCCESS; HE SOUGHT LASTING IMPACT. HIS AFFIRMATIONS EVOLVED INTO A WAY OF LIFE, GUIDING HIM THROUGH CHALLENGES, BOTH PERSONAL AND PROFESSIONAL, THAT FOLLOWED. WHETHER IT WAS OVERCOMING INJURIES, NAVIGATING THE COMPLEXITIES OF HOLLYWOOD, OR CREATING HIS UNIQUE MARTIAL ART, JEET KUNE DO, LEE'S UNWAVERING BELIEF IN HIS OWN POTENTIAL WAS CENTRAL TO HIS JOURNEY.

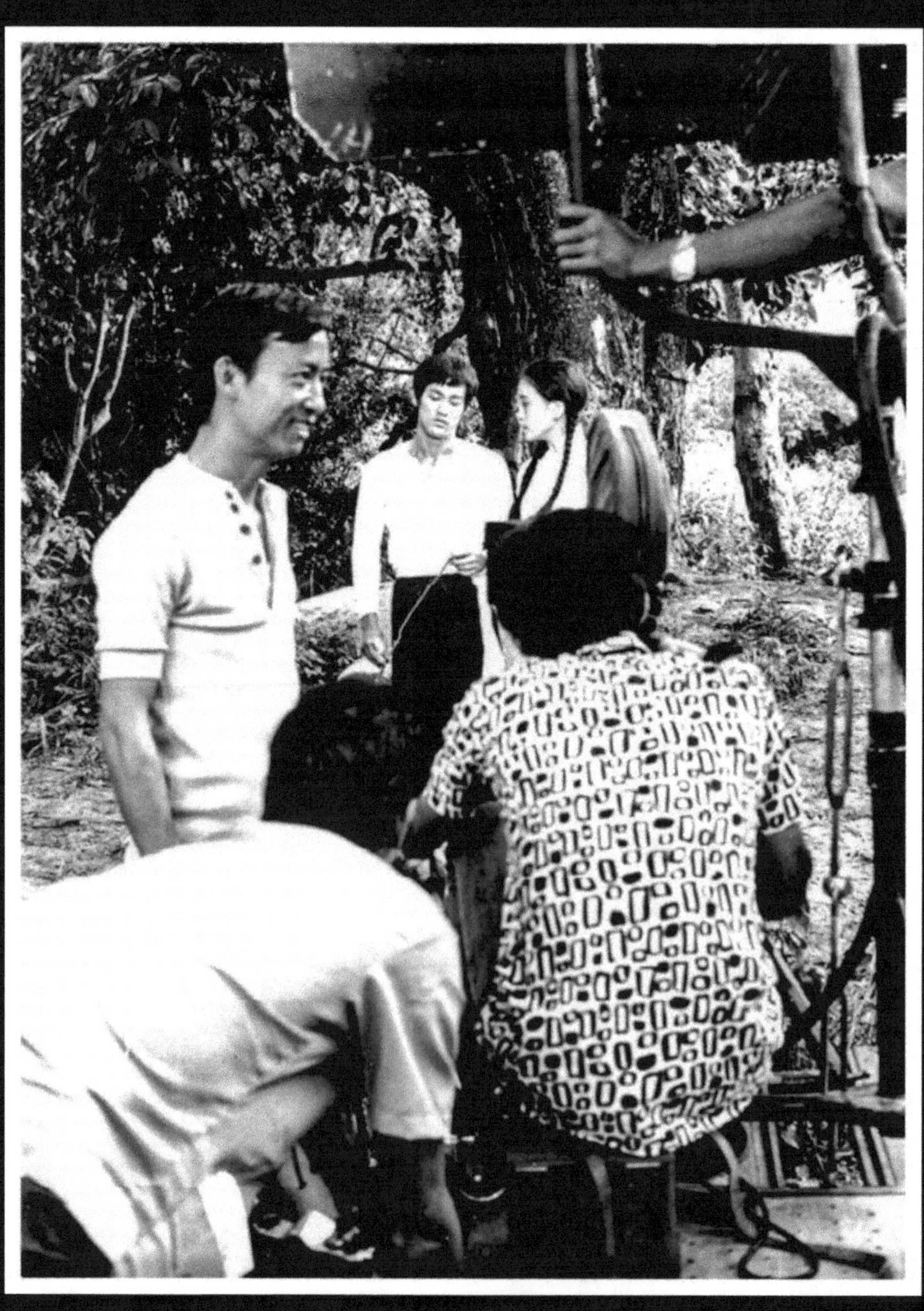

しかし、リーのアファメーションの影響は、彼の最初のブレイクスルーをはるかに超えて広がりまし
た。彼が培った精神的な鍛錬は、人生と武道に対する彼の全哲学の基盤となりました。リーは一時的
な成功に満足せず、持続的な影響を求めました。彼のアファメーションは生活の一部として進化し、
続く個人的および職業的な挑戦を乗り越えるための指針となりました。怪我を克服すること、ハリウ
ッドの複雑さを乗り切ること、あるいは独自の武道である截拳道（ジークンドー）を創り出すことな
ど、リーの揺るぎない自己の可能性への信念は、彼の旅の中心にありました。

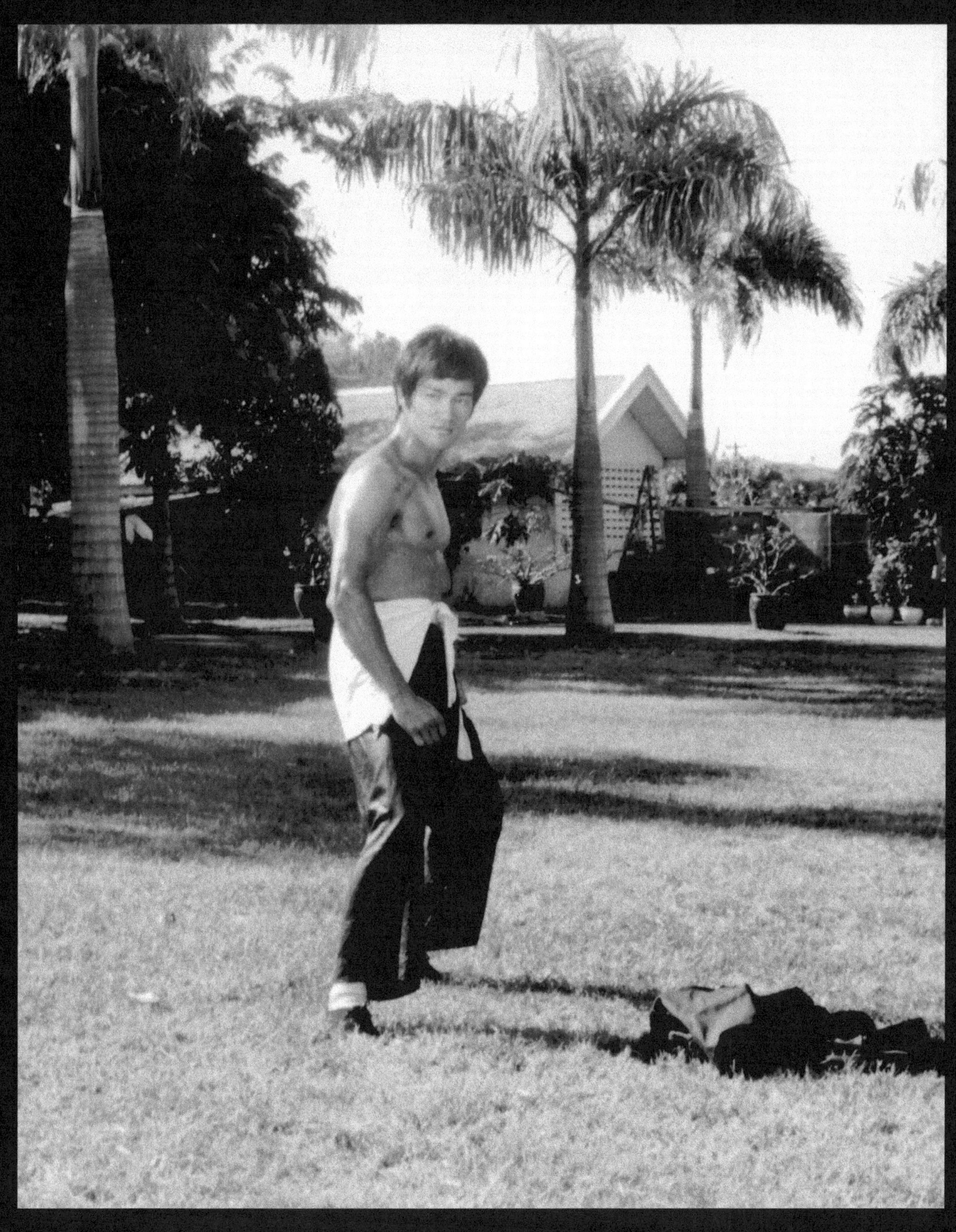

HIS JOURNALS REVEAL THAT EVEN AFTER ACHIEVING GLOBAL FAME, LEE CONTINUED TO REFINE HIS THOUGHTS AND AMBITIONS, ALWAYS PUSHING THE BOUNDARIES OF WHAT HE COULD ACCOMPLISH. HE UNDERSTOOD THAT SUCCESS WAS NOT A DESTINATION BUT A CONTINUOUS JOURNEY OF GROWTH AND SELF-IMPROVEMENT. THIS MINDSET, ROOTED IN HIS AFFIRMATIONS, ENABLED LEE TO LEAVE A LEGACY THAT TRANSCENDS THE SCREEN—A LEGACY THAT CONTINUES TO INSPIRE MILLIONS AROUND THE WORLD TO THIS DAY.

IN THE END, BRUCE LEE'S STORY IS A POWERFUL REMINDER THAT THE PATH TO GREATNESS LIES WITHIN. HIS LIFE ILLUSTRATES THAT WITH THE RIGHT MINDSET, UNWAVERING COMMITMENT, AND THE COURAGE TO PURSUE ONE'S DREAMS, ANYTHING IS POSSIBLE. HIS AFFIRMATIONS WERE MORE THAN JUST WORDS; THEY WERE THE BLUEPRINT FOR A LIFE THAT WOULD LEAVE AN INDELIBLE MARK ON THE WORLD.

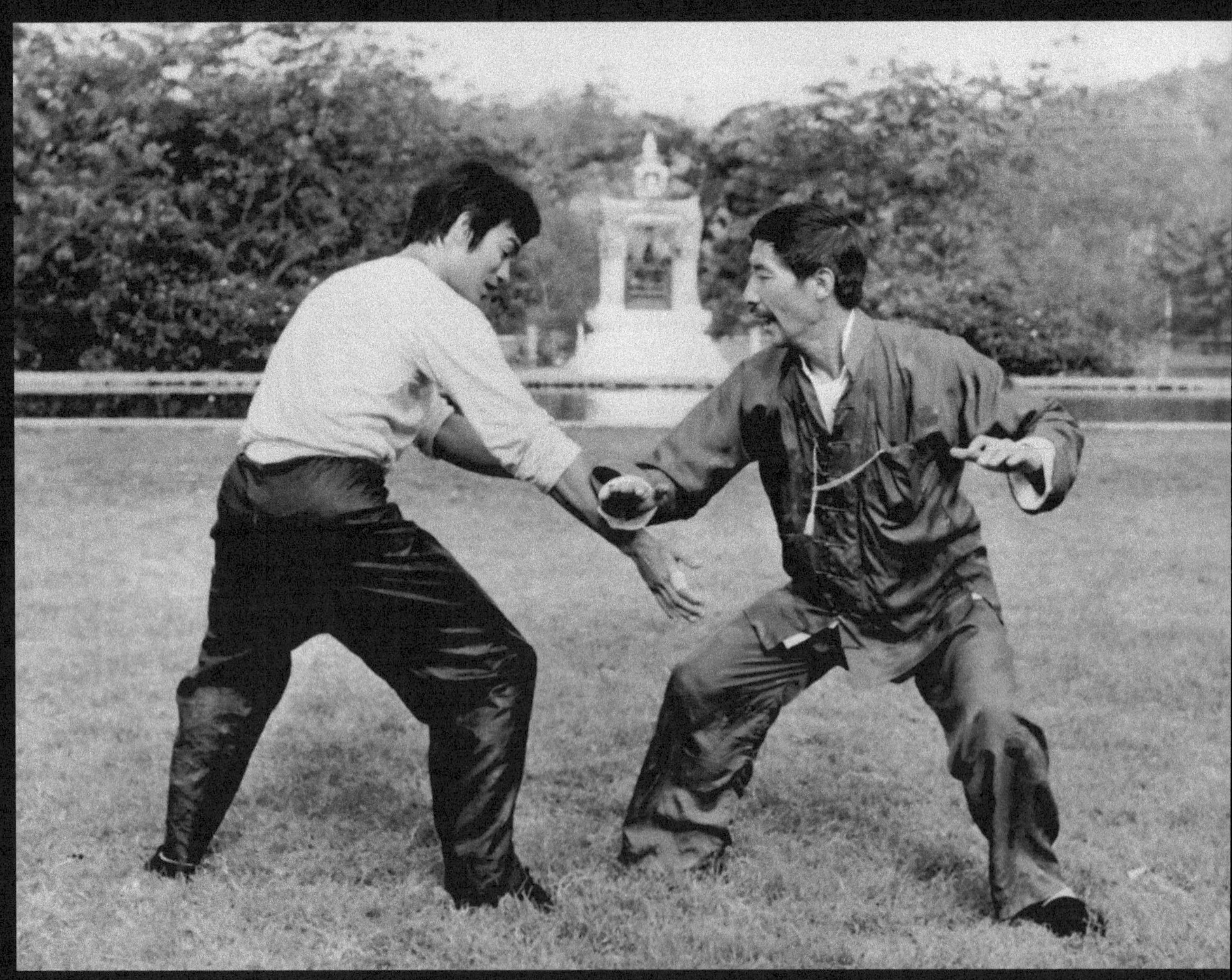

彼の日記からは、世界的な名声を得た後も、リーが自身の考えや野心を磨き続け、常に自分の限界を超えようとしていたことが明らかになります。彼は、成功が目的地ではなく、成長と自己改善の絶え間ない旅であることを理解していました。この心構えが、彼のアファーメーションに根ざしており、スクリーンを超えて残る遺産を築くことを可能にしたのです。その遺産は、今日でも世界中の何百万もの人々にインスピレーションを与え続けています。

最終的に、ブルース・リーの物語は、偉大さへの道が自分の内にあることを強く示しています。彼の人生は、正しい心構え、不動の献身、そして夢を追い求める勇気があれば、何事も可能であることを示しています。彼のアファーメーションは、単なる言葉以上のものであり、世界に消えない印象を残す人生の青写真でもありました

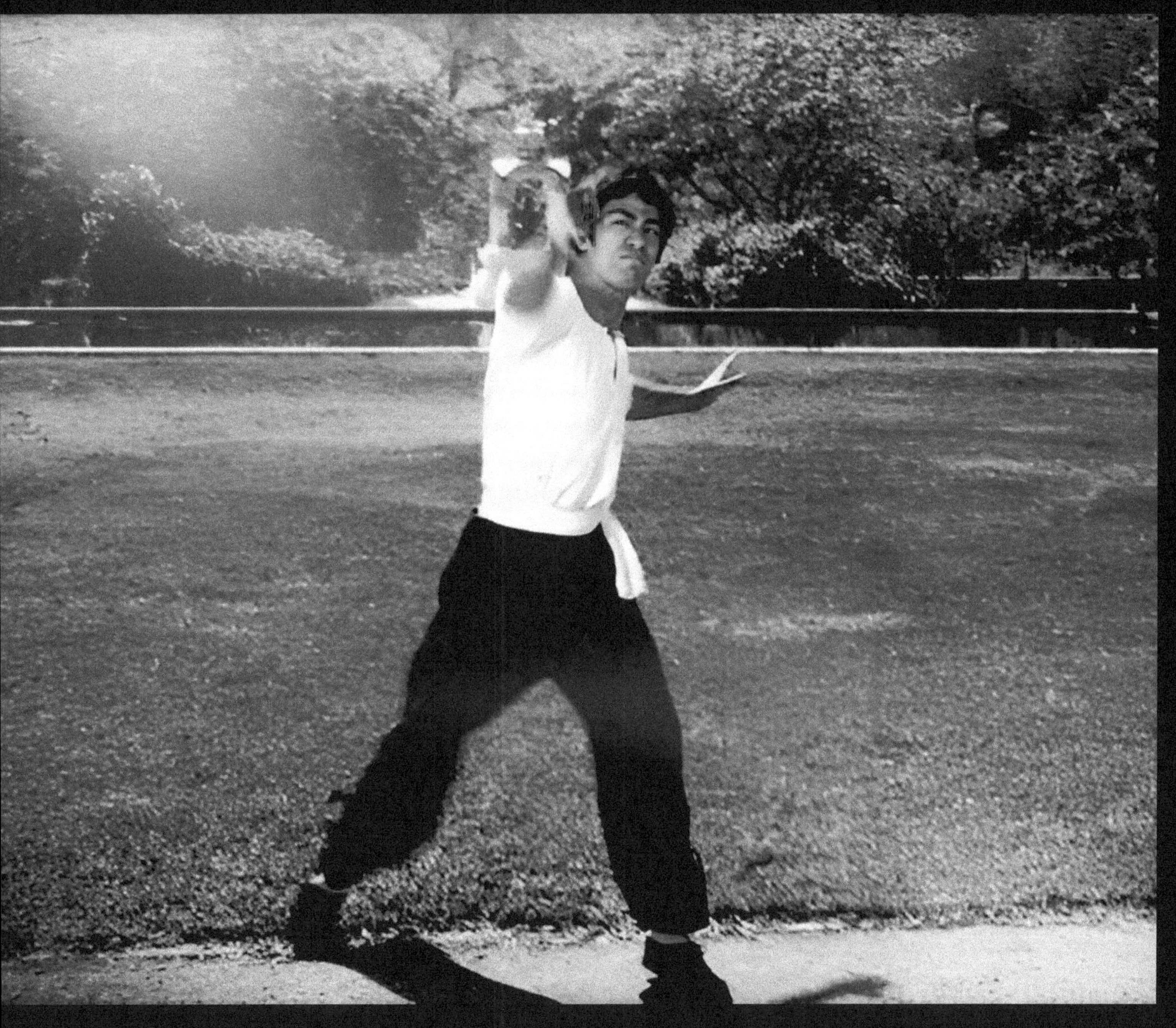

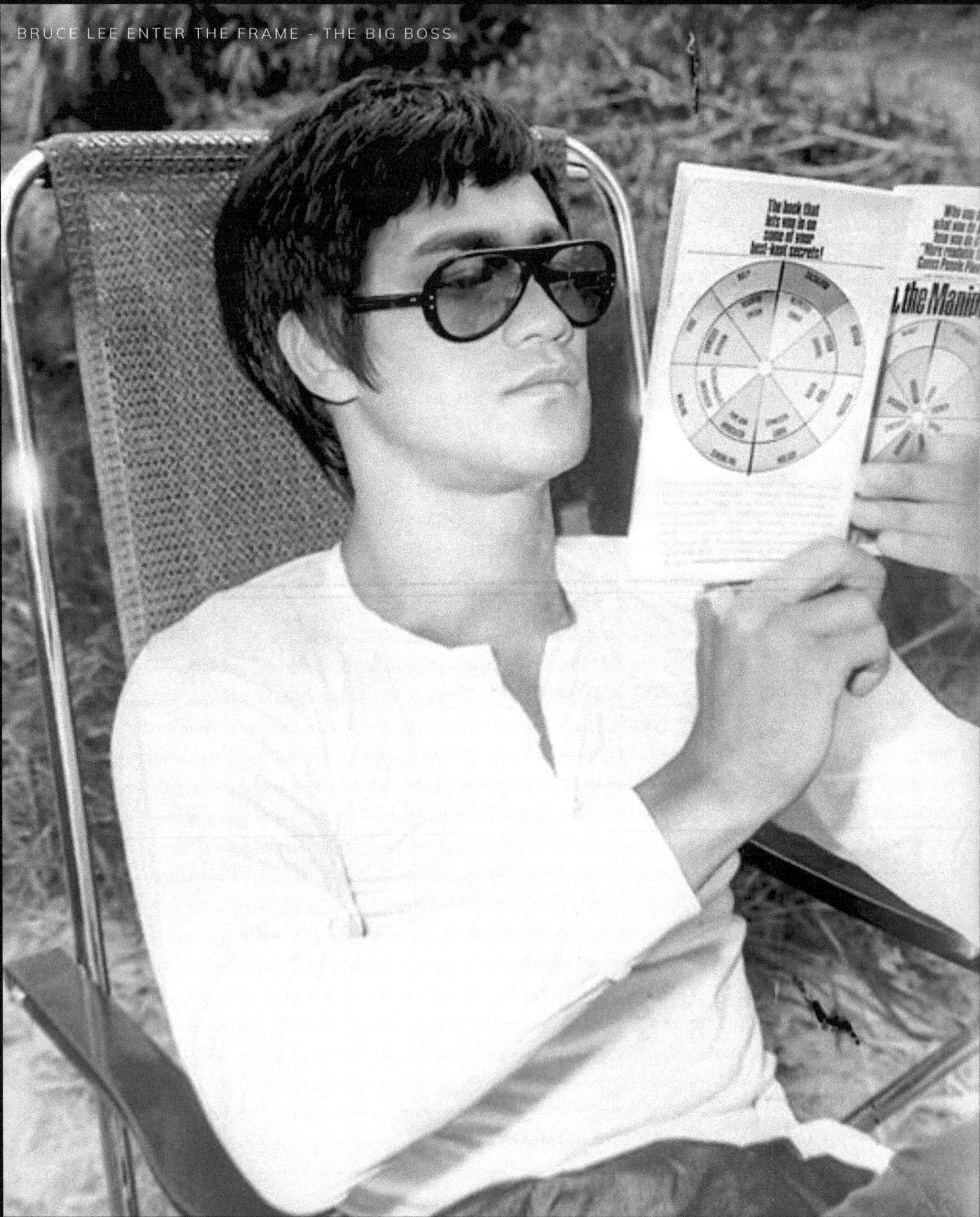
The book that
lets you in on
some of your
best-kept secrets!

THE JOURNAL AFFIRMATIONS OF BRUCE LEE

THE BIG BOSS BRUCE LEE'S MINDSET PHOTO SCRAPBOOK:

N HIS AFFIRMATIONS, LEE DELVED INTO PROFOUND PSYCHOLOGICAL CONCEPTS LIKE WILLPOWER, EMOTION, AND REASON. HE BELIEVED HAT TRUE MASTERY CAME FROM ALIGNING THE MIND AND BODY, AND HIS AFFIRMATIONS WERE A WAY TO STRENGTHEN THIS CONNECTION. OR LEE, WILLPOWER WASN'T JUST ABOUT WANTING SUCCESS; IT WAS ABOUT WILLING IT INTO EXISTENCE THROUGH FOCUSED EFFORT. HE ECOGNIZED THE IMPORTANCE OF BALANCING EMOTION WITH REASON, DERSTANDING THAT WHILE EMOTIONS COULD DRIVE PASSION, IT WAS REASON THAT SHOULD GUIDE ACTIONS.

S HE PREPARED FOR "THE BIG BOSS," LEE'S AFFIRMATIONS BECAME A DAILY RITUAL. HE VISUALIZED HIS SUCCESS, REAFFIRMED HIS OMMITMENT, AND MENTALLY PREPARED HIMSELF AS RIGOROUSLY AS HE DID PHYSICALLY. WHEN THE FILM WAS RELEASED, IT BECAME AN VERNIGHT SENSATION, SETTING BOX OFFICE RECORDS IN HONG KONG.

THIS SUCCESS WAS A TESTAMENT TO LEE'S BELIEF IN THE POWER OF E MIND. HIS AFFIRMATIONS NOT ONLY SHAPED HIS INNER WORLD BUT ALSO HELPED TURN HIS DREAMS INTO REALITY, PROVING THAT TRUE SUCCESS IS ACHIEVED FROM WITHIN.

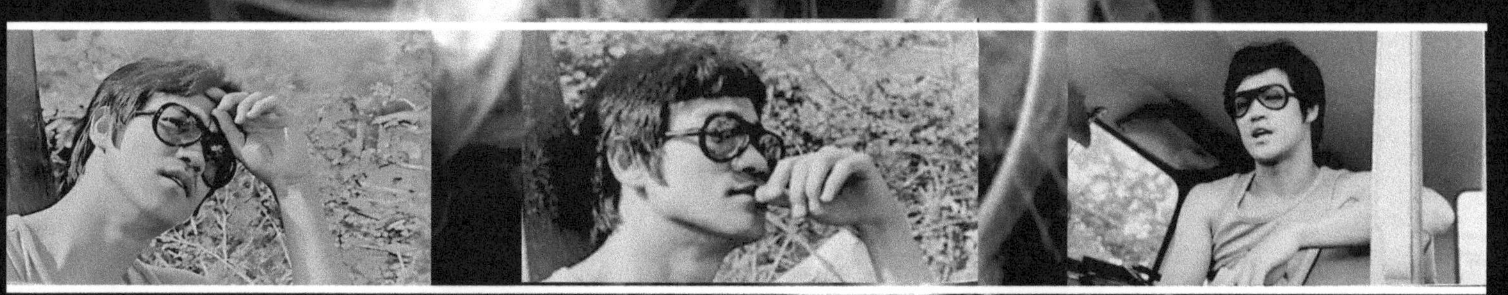

ブルース・リーのアファメーション日記

ブルース・リーが名声を得たのは、特に彼のブレイクスルーとなった映画『ドラゴン危機一発』の役によるものでしたが、その成功は彼の肉体的なスキルだけでなく、強力な精神力にも支えられていました。この映画の公開に至るまで、リーはその広範な日記に見られるように、精神的な鍛錬に深く没頭していました。その中でも、彼のアファメーション（自己宣言）は、彼の成功の重要な要素として際立っています。これらは単なるモチベーションの言葉ではなく、彼の目標と信念を明確に宣言したものでした。

彼のアファメーションの中で、リーは意志力、感情、理性といった深遠な心理学的概念に深く踏み込みました。彼は、真の達成は心と身体の調和から生まれると信じており、アファメーションはこの結びつきを強化するための手段でした。リーにとって、意志力は単に成功を望むことではなく、集中した努力によってそれを現実にすることでした。彼は感情と理性のバランスの重要性を認識し、感情が情熱を駆り立てる一方で、行動を導くべきは理性であると理解していました。

『ドラゴン危機一発』の準備を進める中で、リーのアファメーションは日々の習慣となりました。彼は自らの成功を視覚化し、コミットメントを再確認し、身体的な準備と同じくらい精神的な準備にも力を入れました。この映画が公開されたとき、瞬く間に大ヒットし、香港の興行収入記録を打ち立てました。

この成功は、心の力を信じるリーの信念の証です。彼のアファメーションは、彼の内なる世界を形作るだけでなく、彼の夢を現実に変える助けとなり、真の成功は内面から達成されることを証明しました。

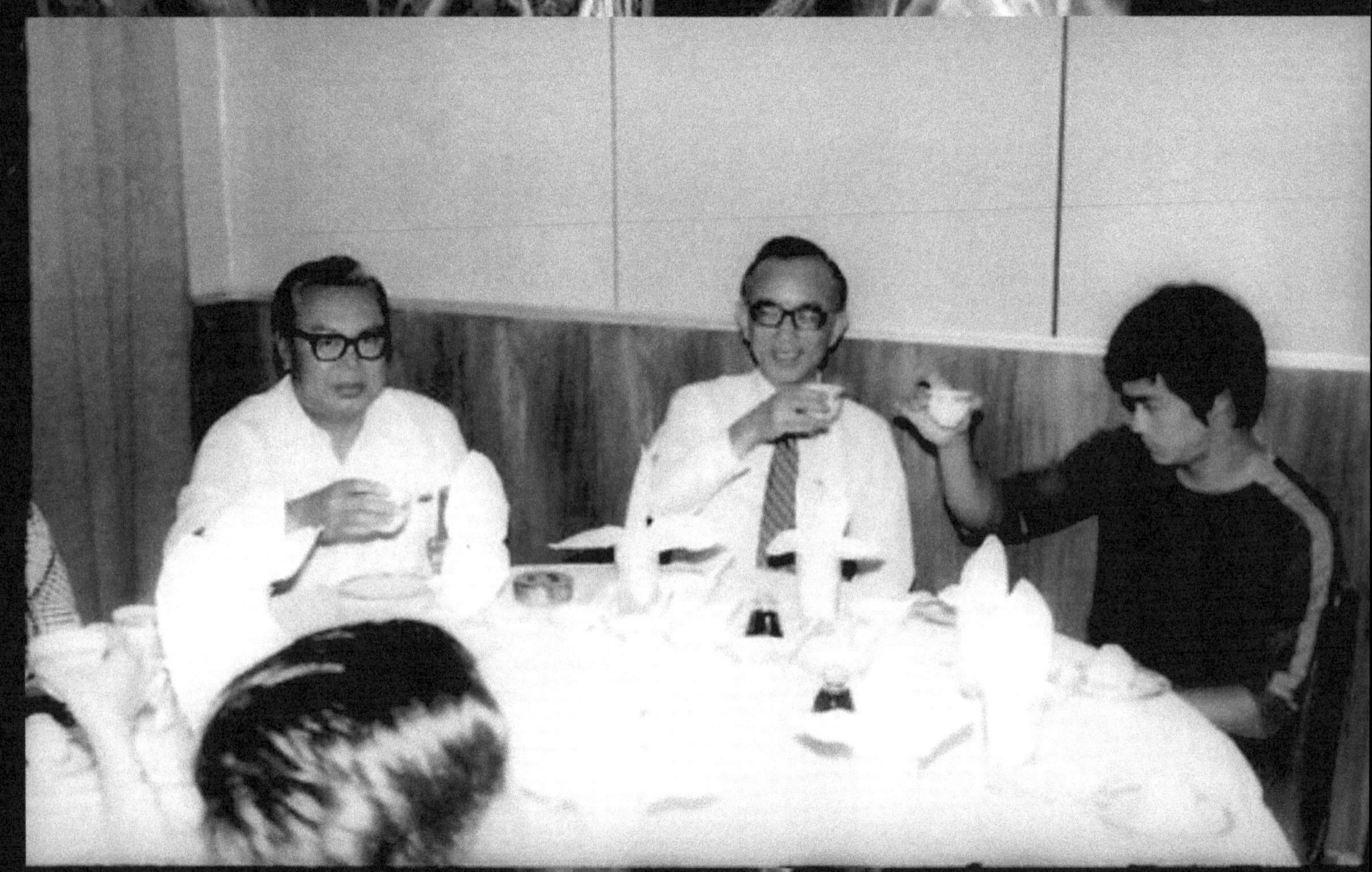

My Definite Chief Aim

I, Bruce Lee, will be the first highest paid Oriental super star in the United States. In return I will give the most exciting performances and render the best of quality in the capacity of an actor. Starting 1970 I will achieve world fame and from then onward till the end of 1980 I will have in my possession $10,000,000. I will live the way I please and achieve inner harmony and happiness.

Bruce Lee
Jan 1969

THE EARLIEST RECORD THE PUBLIC HAS ABOUT HIS AFFIRMATIONS DATES TO 1968 WHEN HE WAS ONLY 28 YEARS OLD – A TIME IN WHICH HE WAS HIGHLY AMBITIOUS ABOUT WHAT HE WANTED TO ACCOMPLISH PERSONALLY AND PROFESSIONALLY. SO MUCH SO THAT HE PENNED THE FOLLOWING PAGE IN 1969 AT AGE 29 REGARDING HIS CHIEF AIM;

ブルース・リーのアファメーション日記

公に彼のアファメーションが記録された最も早い時期は、彼が28歳だった1968年のことです。この時期、彼は個人としても、またプロとしても、成し遂げたいことに対して非常に野心的でした。それほどまでに、彼は1969年、29歳のときに、次のように彼の主な目標について記しました。

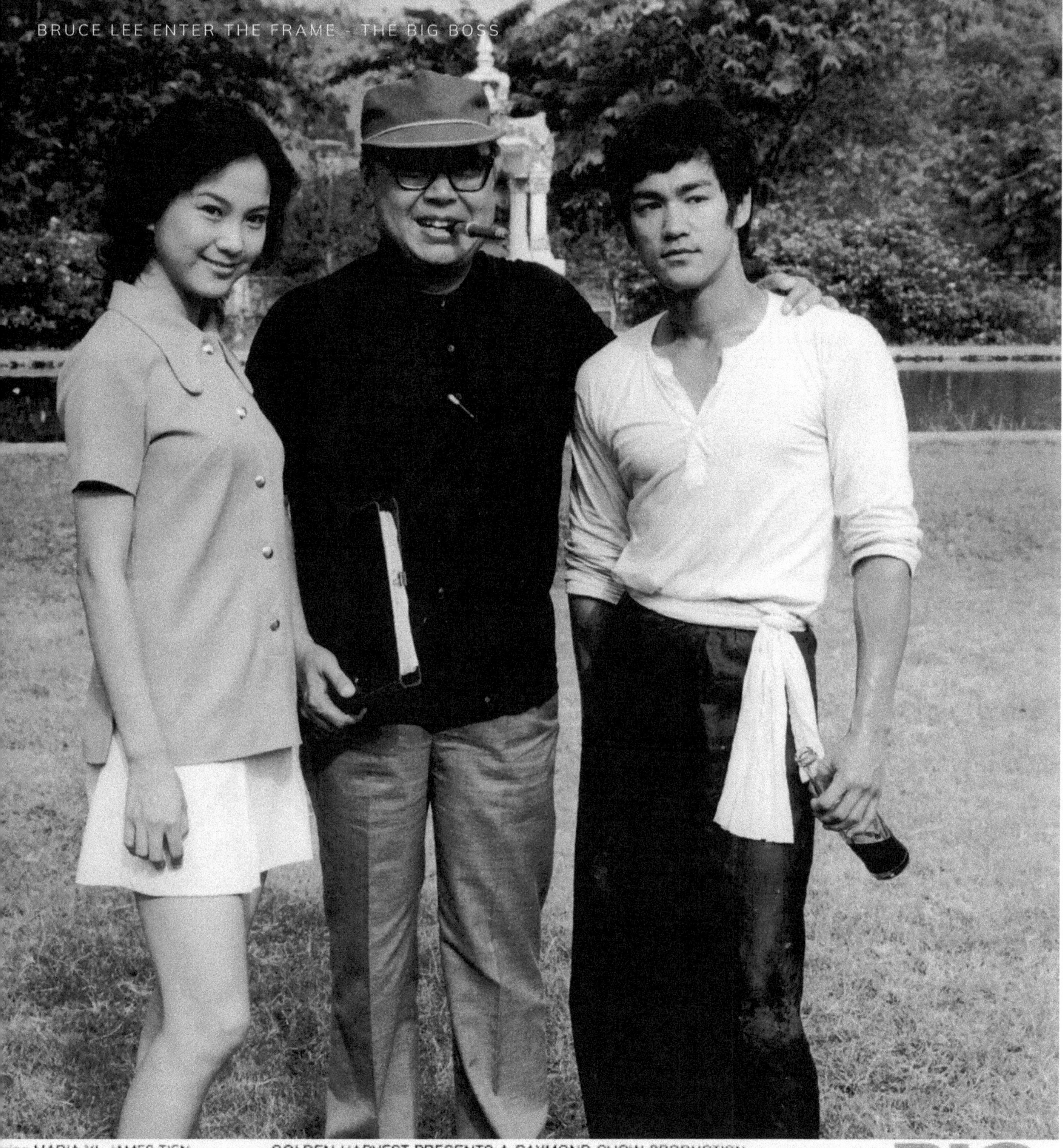
ring MARIA YI   JAMES TIEN
st appearance by NORA MIAO
duced by RAYMOND CHOW
tten and Directed by LO WEI
GOLDEN HARVEST PRESENTS A RAYMOND CHOW PRODUCTION
BRUCE LEE in THE BIG BOSS
e and Colour
© 1971 Golden Harvest (Hong Kong) Limited

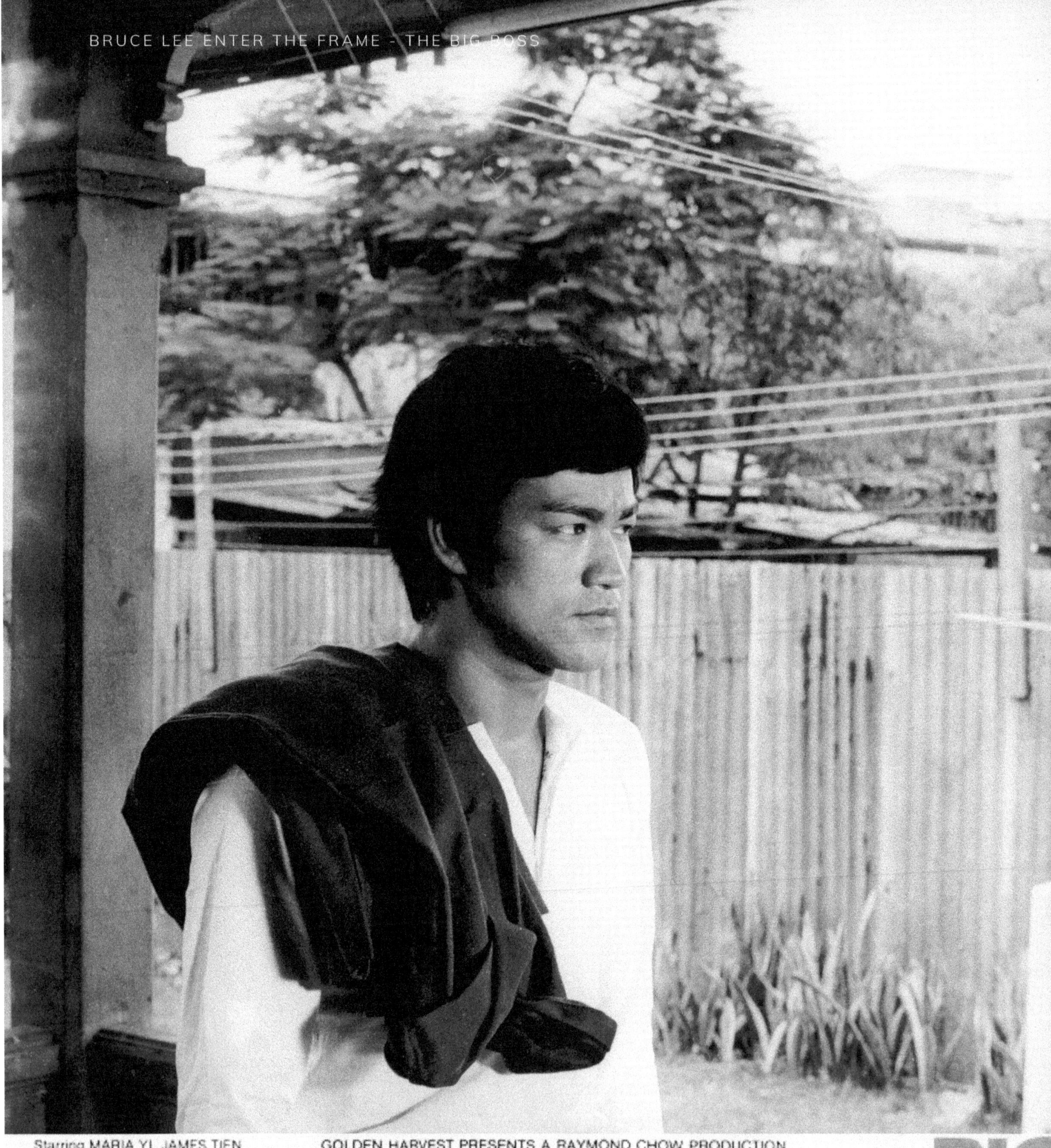
Starring MARIA YI JAMES TIEN
Guest appearance by NORA MIAO
Produced by RAYMOND CHOW
Written and Directed by LO WEI
GOLDEN HARVEST PRESENTS A RAYMOND CHOW PRODUCTION
BRUCE LEE in THE BIG BOSS
Scope and Colour
©1971 Golden Harvest (Hong Kong) Limited

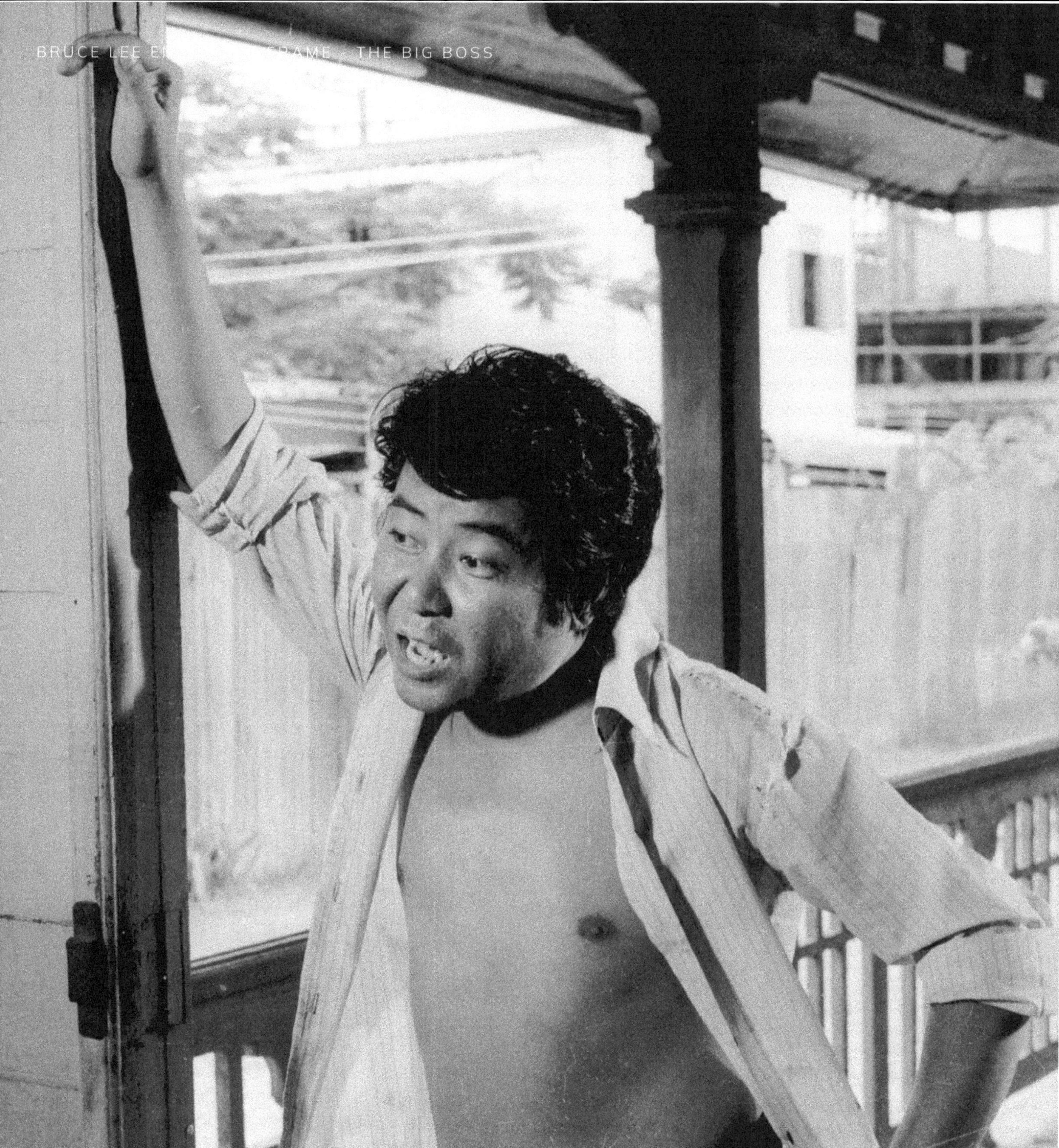
arring MARIA YI JAMES TIEN
uest appearance by NORA MIAO
oduced by RAYMOND CHOW
ritten and Directed by LO WEI
ope and Colour
GOLDEN HARVEST PRESENTS A RAYMOND CHOW PRODUCTION
BRUCE LEE in THE BIG BOSS
©1971 Golden Harvest (Hong Kong) Limited

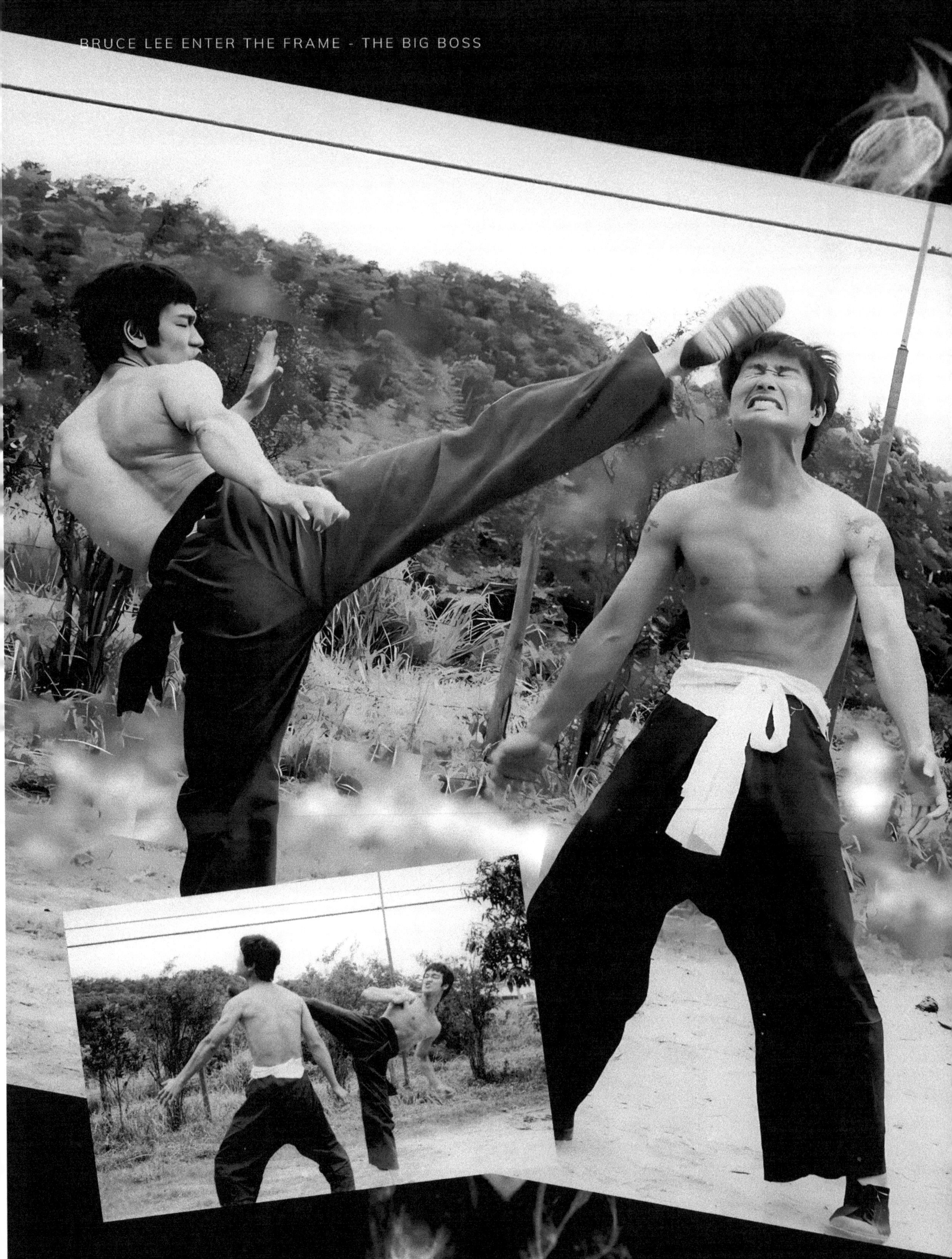

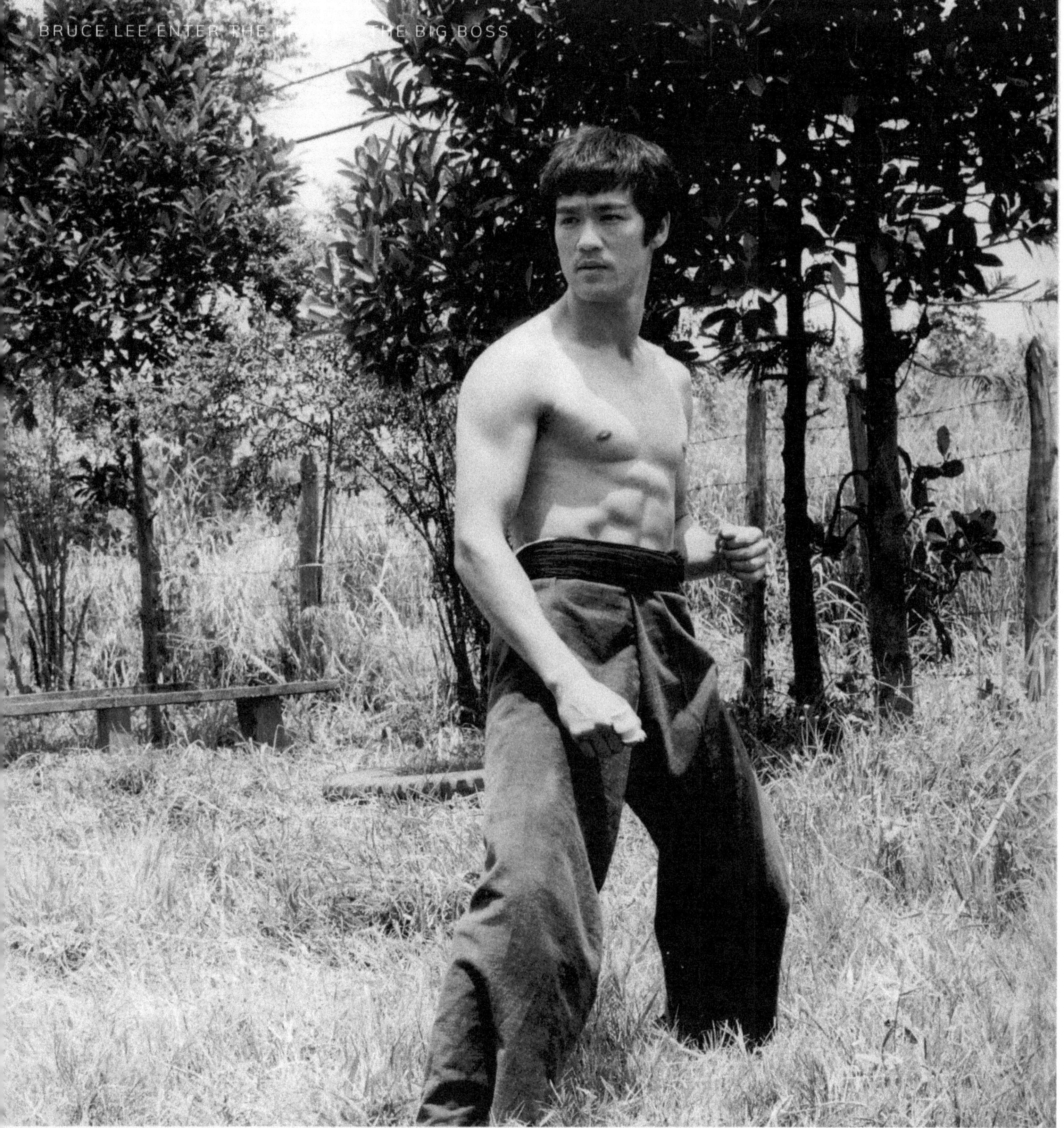
BRUCE LEE ENTER THE   THE BIG BOSS
arring MARIA YI JAMES TIEN
est appearance by NORA MIAO
oduced by RAYMOND CHOW
ritten and Directed by LO WEI
GOLDEN HARVEST PRESENTS A RAYMOND CHOW PRODUCTION
BRUCE LEE in THE BIG BOSS
©1971 Golden Harvest (Hong Kong) Limited
pe and Colour

Starring MARIA YI JAMES TIEN
Guest appearance by NORA MIAO
Produced by RAYMOND CHOW
Written and Directed by LO WEI
GOLDEN HARVEST PRESENTS A RAYMOND CHOW PRODUCTION
BRUCE LEE in
THE BIG BOSS
Scope and Colour
©1971 Golden Harvest (Hong Kong) Limited

Starring MARIA YI JAMES TIEN
Guest appearance by NORA MIAO
Produced by RAYMOND CHOW
Written and Directed by LO WEI
GOLDEN HARVEST PRESENTS A RAYMOND CHOW PRODUCTION
BRUCE LEE in THE BIG BOSS
©1971 Golden Harvest (Hong Kong) Limited
Scope and Colour

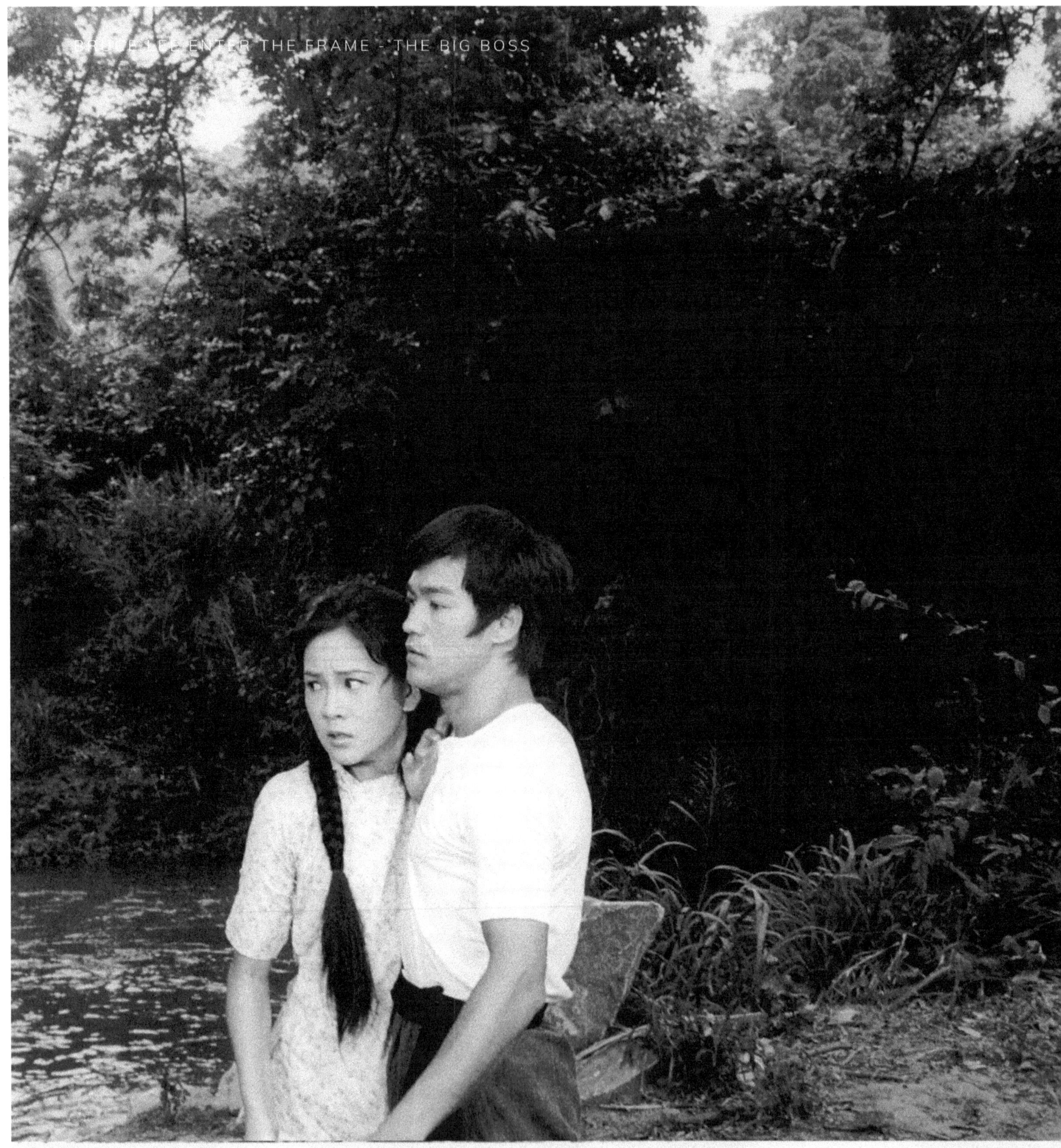

BRUCE LEE - ENTER THE FRAME - THE BIG BOSS

Starring MARIA YI JAMES TIEN
Guest appearance by NORA MIAO
Produced by RAYMOND CHOW
Written and Directed by LO WEI

GOLDEN HARVEST PRESENTS A RAYMOND CHOW PRODUCTION

BRUCE LEE in THE BIG BOSS

Scope and Colour

©1971 Golden Harvest (Hong Kong) Limited

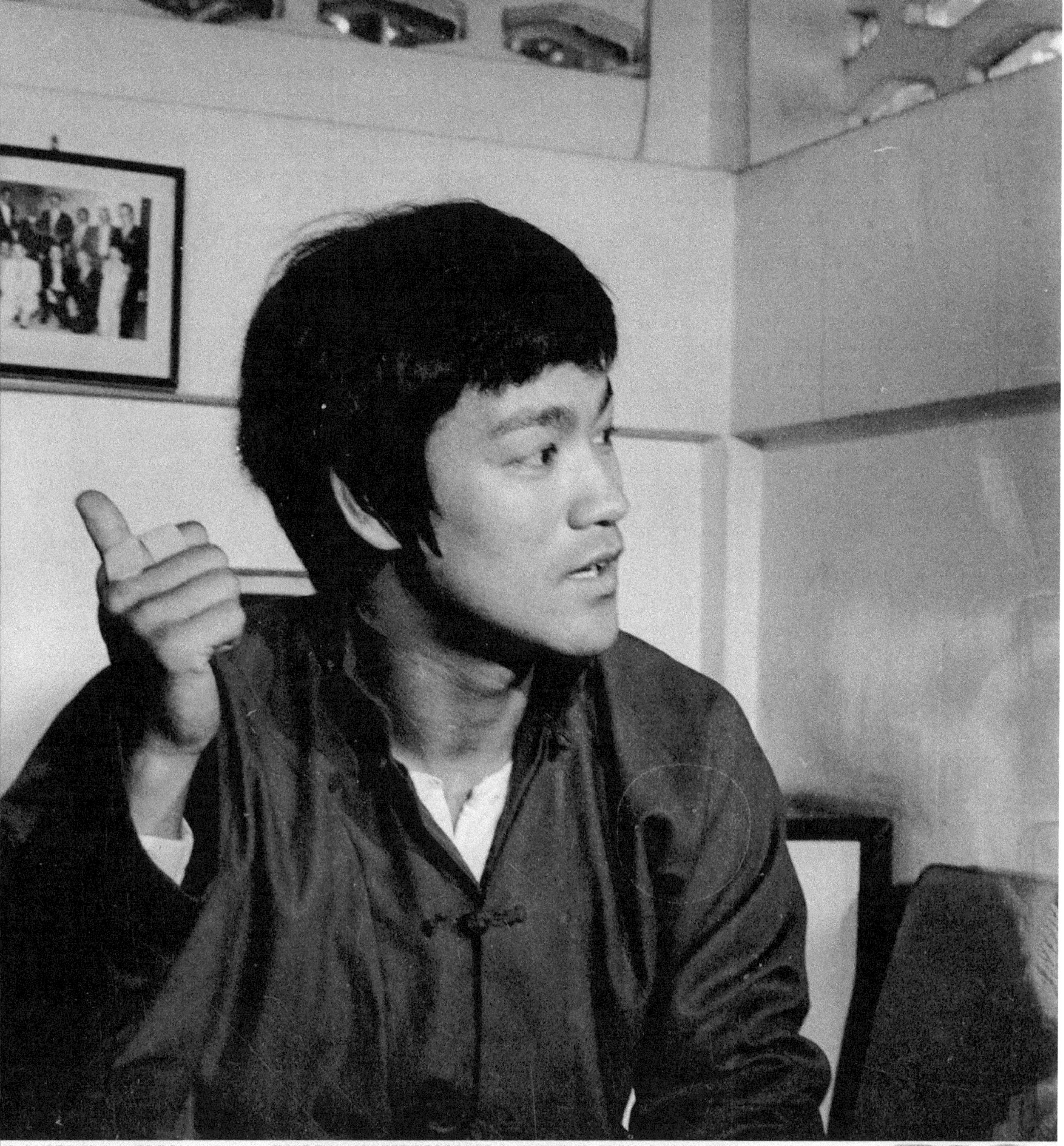
rring MARIA YI JAMES TIEN
st appearance by NORA MIAO
duced by RAYMOND CHOW
tten and Directed by LO WEI
GOLDEN HARVEST PRESENTS A RAYMOND CHOW PRODUCTION
BRUCE LEE in THE BIG BOSS
e and Colour
©1971 Golden Harvest (Hong Kong) Limited

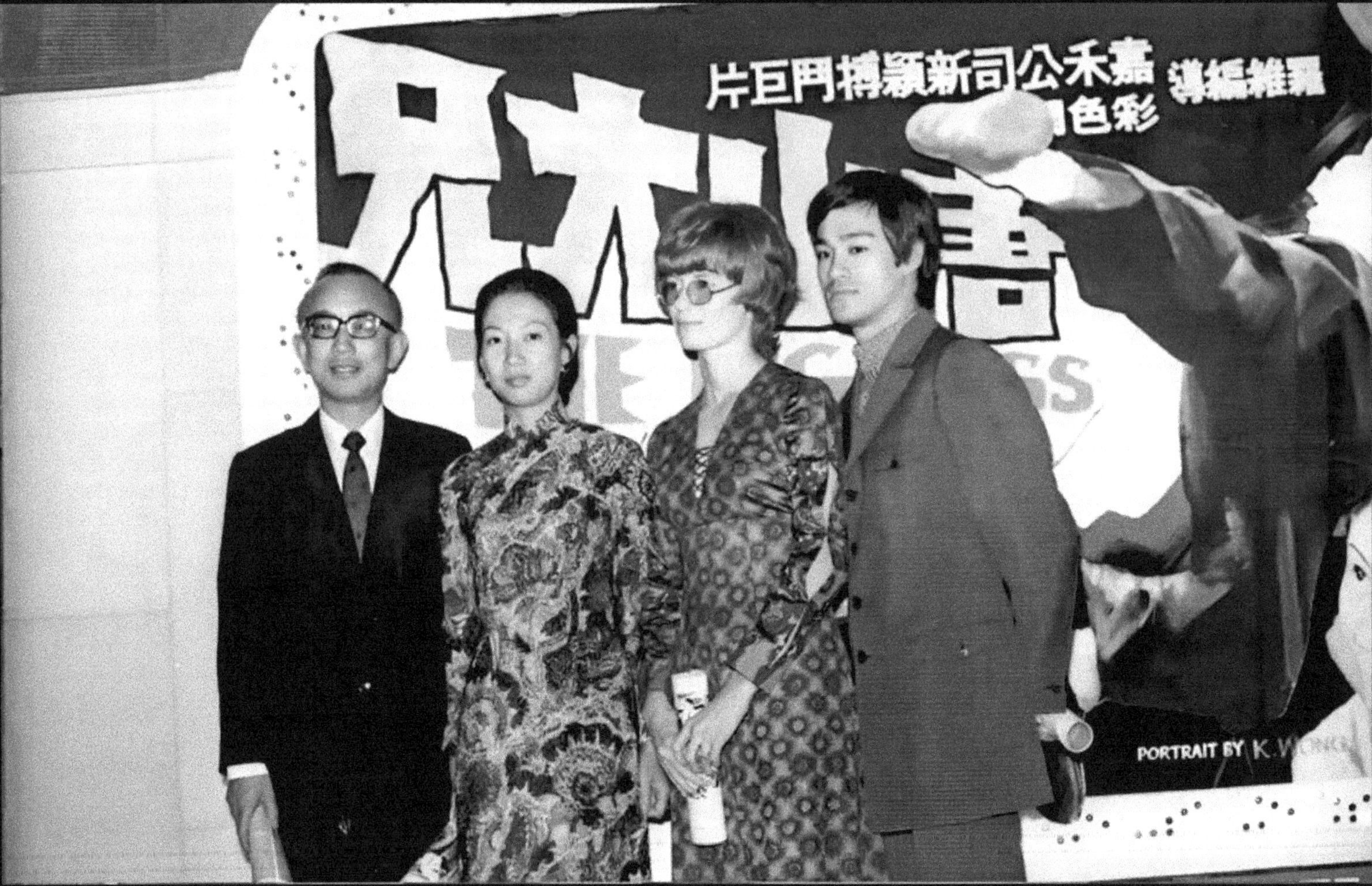

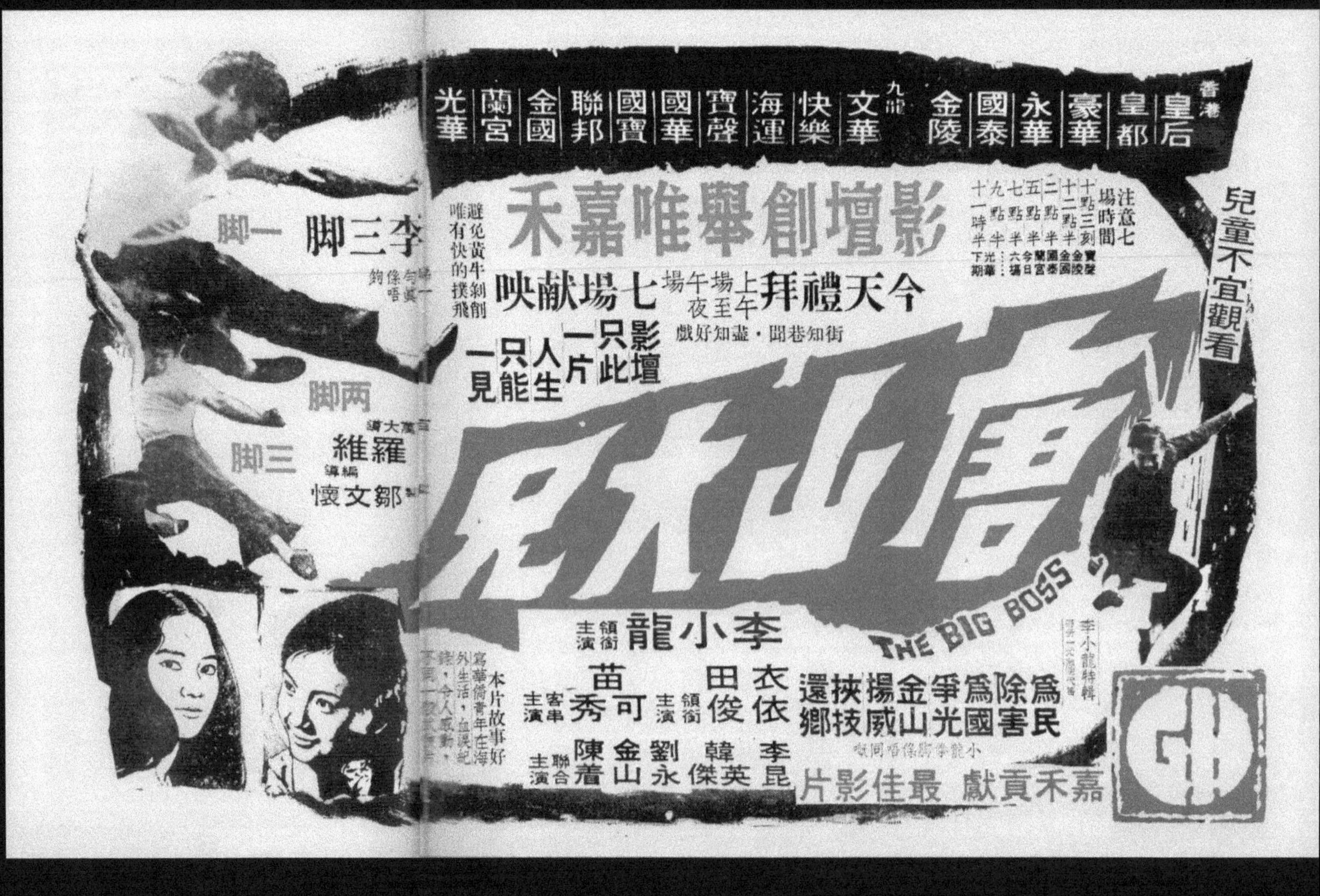

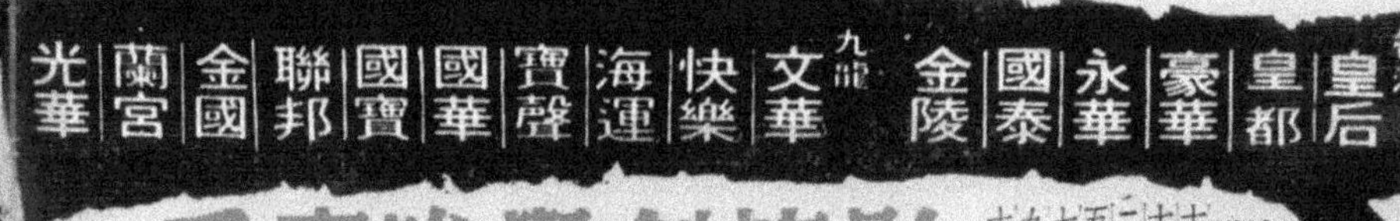
嘉禾公司新穎搏鬥巨片
羅維編導
彩色闊
PORTRAIT BY K. WONG
香港 皇后 皇都 豪華 永華 國泰 金陵 九龍 文華 快樂 海運 寶聲 國華 國寶 聯邦 金國 蘭宮 光華
影壇創舉唯一嘉禾
今天禮拜上場午場七場獻映
兒童不宜觀看
李三脚 一脚
維羅 導編 鄒文懷
脚兩
脚三
唐山大兄
THE BIG BOSS
領銜主演 李小龍
苗可秀 田俊 衣依
陳秀金 劉永 韓英傑 李昆
嘉禾貢獻 最佳影片
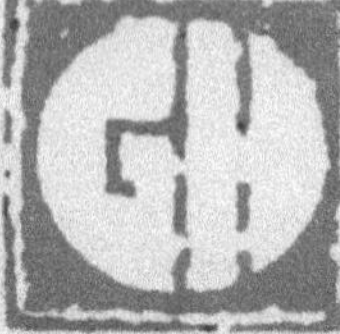

www.ingramcontent.com/pod-product-compliance
Lightning Source LLC
Chambersburg PA
CBHW040904070726
47599CB00038B/2299